# Careers in Advertising

BY EVA LEDERMAN

*Random House, Inc.*
*New York*
*www.randombouse.com*

*The Princeton Review*

Princeton Review Publishing, L.L.C.
2315 Broadway, Second Floor
New York, NY 10024
E-mail: info@review.com

ISSN 1522-0451

ISBN 0-375-75091-6

Editor: Gretchen Feder

Designer: Adam Hurwitz

Production Editor: Kristen Azzara

Manufactured in the United States of America on partially recycled paper.

9 8 7 6 5 4 3 2 1

First Edition

# Contents

In any industry there are certain keys that will help you get past the front door. How do you find these keys? How do you ensure that you stay once you've made it in? How do you know which doors to knock on?

A complete list of agencies in the following cities to aid you in your job and internship search.

An extensive list of what the professionals read and what web sites they visit to give you the inside track on the industry.

# *Foreword*

## BY SHELLY LAZARUS
### Chairman and CEO, Ogilvy & Mather Worldwide

Nearly thirty years ago, when I was in college, I knew absolutely nothing about advertising—let alone imagined I'd have a lifelong career in this industry or someday become the Chairman and CEO of a worldwide advertising agency. I stumbled into a career in advertising by accident. One weekend while I was attending Smith College, I grabbed the opportunity to get a ride home to New York with a friend so that I could see my fiance—my future husband. My friend was going to a career day sponsored by Advertising Women of New York and I tagged along. That happy accident was the beginning of my lifetime love of advertising.

But I don't downplay how fortunate I was to fall into advertising. After all, at that time it was still very difficult for women to break into business. We were told by companies that we couldn't be hired for sales jobs because the sample case was too heavy for us to carry around, or that they'd have to give the job to a man because he was also supporting a family.

Advertising was one of the first businesses to be open to women for a simple reason that still holds true today and applies to anyone. Advertising is a business based on ideas. A good idea is a good idea. Period. Whether it originates from a man or a woman, in the board room or the mail room, in creative or accounting. That's why I love this business. No matter who you are or what your educational background is, you have an equal opportunity to come up with a big idea.

In fact, at Ogilvy & Mather we count on diversity. I always find it interesting to note that our people come from all sorts of fields of study—philosophy, psychology, history, music, art, anthropology. Maybe it's not so surprising. Advertising is, after all, an act of culture.

Advertising is also a business in which things are always changing. It's dynamic. There is no guarantee that things in the morning will be the same in the afternoon. There is never a dull moment. If you like that kind of adventure in your day, I promise that you'll never be bored when you work in advertising.

It's probably easier than ever to make that promise because the business has changed so much in thirty years. It's not just about 30-second films or making a print ad. Today we are in the business of building brands—and because a brand is created from the cumulative effect of a variety of consumer impressions, our business is more diverse than ever. Exciting avenues are open beyond the traditional slots for "creatives" and "suits." There are rich careers to be made in direct marketing, planning and research, alternative media, and interactive technology. And all of these disciplines are evolving, too, as we explore new and effective ways to reach our clients' target markets.

Perhaps I'm biased, but I believe there's a place for every kind of talent in advertising today. And I can assure you that, if the business I just described interests you, your career in advertising will certainly offer some of the most rewarding and fascinating years of your life.

# *Introduction*

At the Superbowl's two-minute warning, every advertising professional in the country is glued to the set: the commercial being aired costs nearly $1 million to produce, the price tag on the 30-second time slot is equally expensive, and 80 million people around the world are watching. Is it brilliant? Whose idea was it? In this high-profile business driven by creativity, competition for careers will always be fierce.

The current outlook for jobs in advertising is cautiously optimistic. Advertising tracks the overall economy very closely. When the economy is up, businesses invest more money in advertising, and when the economy is down, advertising is one of the first expenses to be cut. Advertising expenditures rose in 1998 and are expected to rise again. The general economy has strengthened and stabilized, suggesting a pattern of modest growth over the next several years.

However, the economy is now driven by slavish devotion to efficiency and accountability. "Leanness" is the watchword of the day and fewer numbers of people are forced to work harder than ever, with the constant fear of ultimately being replaced by technology. This has both positive and negative implications for beginners. On the upside, many agencies are lean as a result of painful downsizing during the recession. They need more help and don't want to pay a lot of money. Hungry juniors who can get the job done have an opportunity to step into substantive positions. On the downside, there are fewer levels on the ladder, including fewer junior and trainee positions—in fact, "training" as a concept has fared poorly in the reign of efficiency.

The technological revolution is radically changing the face of the advertising business. Although the technology itself has been present for some time, it is only within the past couple of years that agencies have become fully equipped to allow for intra-agency as well as international exchange of information. Agencies are globally networked by modem, fax, and the Internet and use complex and powerful new software systems. TBWA/Chiat Day now has a "virtual office." Employees have lockers to store their personal belongings and a large room full of desks has replaced individual offices. These transformations have a significant effect on junior-level positions.

The traditional concept of "paying your dues" has always been a part of the advertising business. Today, technology has forever changed the nature of that concept. Back in 1955, Tom Clark, president and Chief Operating Officer of BBDO, sorted mail. Walter Kaprielian, president and CEO of Ketchum Advertising, started as a photostat clerk at BBDO. Richard Levine, chairman of the former Levine, Huntley, Schmidt & Beaver, was "the office boy," and copied radio scripts on the mimeograph machine for three hours a day.

E-mail now eliminates the need for phone calls and messages. Faxing has replaced sending and receiving hard copies through the postal service. Xeroxing and mailing documents have been superseded by the ability to transfer files electronically. Systems of information retrieval and storage eliminate the need for filing. Desktop publishing has replaced paste-up and mechanicals. As a result, juniors will no longer be taking messages, mailing, and typing. Now they will manage databases, search for and retrieve information—often via the Internet, and operate complex computer systems.

*Careers in Advertising* is designed to equip you with strategies to give you a competitive edge in the rapidly changing advertising industry. The purpose of the book is twofold: to provide unique inside information gleaned from in-depth interviews with successful young professionals and to examine the impact of the information revolution on the advertising business.

Part One of the book comprises six interviews with young advertising executives who share their insights and experiences on overcoming the obstacles to obtaining an entry-level job, surviving the first year, and working your way toward a promotion. They offer specific job search techniques and inside tips on breaking into the business through their personal and inspirational stories. These savvy young professionals have the most current perspective on what it takes to launch a successful career in the world of advertising as it enters a new era.

This section also covers the major departments of an advertising agency: account management, creative, media, planning, traffic, and new business. It describes the work of each department and the ways in which technology has affected the division's operations. Each chapter also presents opportunities, describes required skills, and offers advice on the job search process. In addition, Chapter 7 addresses corporate advertising and life on the other side of the fence—working in the in-house advertising department of a major corporation.

Part Two addresses opportunities in agencies that students don't often consider: healthcare, ethnic, specialty, interactive, direct marketing, sales promotion, and small agencies. While this section offers career advice specific to each of these industries, which are growing quickly and exploding with new opportunities, it also offers valuable insights into advertising as a whole.

Healthcare agencies have big-budget clients who generate a great deal of advertising. Junior people often start out with more responsibility than they would typically have at a consumer agency and salaries are generally higher. Small agencies allow you the opportunity to wear many different hats. The divisions between departments in small agencies are blurred, and you can become intimately involved in the advertising process and learn it from the ground up. Although you may start out in an administrative capacity, you will no doubt assume other responsibilities quickly when manpower is in short supply. Though clients and budgets are generally smaller, there is a more personal feel to working with a small, tightly knit group.

Direct response is an explosive field. The infomercial has been elevated to an art form, and with more than 80 television stations it is now possible to target a highly specific audience. Most large agencies have subsidiary direct response and promotion agencies that work closely with the parent companies and their clients.

Cyberagencies are revolutionizing the advertising industry as radio, television, and magazines become interactive. With the development of direct TV, laser disks, and online communications, we are witnessing a new breed of consumer who has complete control over media consumption—one who selects from more than 500 television channels and video on demand, reads a customized daily newspaper, and browses through cyberspace. Advertisers are clamoring to jump on the bandwagon as interactivity and personalized persuasion become the name of the game. Cyberagencies are attracting hot young talent, offering higher pay, faster promotions, and the opportunity to explore a dynamic new world of advertising.

"The easiest way to get into advertising," said Charles Rabkin, a long-time ad man, "is to have your father buy the agency." Well, if you're like most of us, you'll need to send a letter and resume. This is the topic of Part Three, which offers a rare, inside look into the hiring process direct from the source. Regina Leonard, associate director of human resources at BBDO Worldwide, takes you through the process of resume writing and interviewing. Your resume needs to set you apart from the crowd and must communicate your own "unique selling proposition." It also must link your skills and experience with your job interest, a tough thing to pull off without a lengthy career history. What sets you apart? What is unique about what you've done in the past and what you are capable of doing for an agency in the future? Before you earn the chance to sell an agency's products, you have to show that you can sell yourself.

Regina also discusses the art of interviewing. What are some typical questions? What types of unorthodox questions will make your head spin? This chapter dissects the interviewing process to help you turn a winning interview into a job offer.

What types of skills do you need to compete today? And how will technology reshape your career in the future? Computer skills and savvy will certainly help you get your foot in the door, but those skills are only part of the package. Although people in advertising have an interest in their field, they have a greater interest in the world around them. Life experience does count in advertising. It shows that you are interested in how the world works and changes. Advertising is a business made up of a variety of different disciplines—psychology, sociology, literature, history, fine arts. And there is no formal training for understanding life. If the advertising world isn't ready for you yet, work on broadening your horizons. "Become a compulsive observer of the human condition," recommends Ron Hoff, president of Ron Hoff & Associates. Travel. Read. Go to museums. Go to McDonald's. Look, listen, and learn. Tom Messner, partner of Messner Vetere Berger McNamee Schmetterer is an ex-postal worker. Helayne Spivak, creative head of Ammirati & Puris, is an ex-pattern cutter. Alex Kroll, former chairman of Young & Rubicam, was a professional football player before he became a copy trainee and eventually CEO. One "right" way to break into advertising doesn't exist. This book will help you discover your own route and maximize your chance of success.

# PART ONE

# *The Traditional Departments*

The traditional ad agency is divided into several different, but equally important departments. Where would you best fit? What skills are required? How can you land a job in your department of choice? How has technology changed the face of these departments? Follow six young professionals as they explain how they made it and tell you how to get the job you want in the department where you belong.

# *Account Management:*
# *Conducting the Orchestra*

## PAM KEEHN, ACCOUNT MANAGER
### TBWA/Chiat Day

If an advertising agency was an orchestra, the account team would be the conductor, interacting with the players and directing the process. Account managers work with the client to develop advertising goals and strategies and then direct the agency resources to ensure that the final product meets those objectives.

Account management involves several steps. The first is to listen to what customers have to say about the product, what they need, and what differentiates the product from others. The second step is to develop an advertising strategy out of that product analysis. This step is usually the joint responsibility of the account manager and the planner. "You do a lot of consumer research, you listen to people, and then you write a [creative] brief that covers everything from the target audience to the competition to what we have to do to support the proposition we're putting forth," says Pam Keehn, account manager at TBWA/Chiat Day, one of Los Angeles' most cutting-edge creative agencies.

The creative brief has five components: the target audience, the business

> "Account managers are the people responsible for the total delivery of an agency's services. They are the leaders, coordinators, and administrators of the teams assigned to clients. A skilled account manager has an enormous impact on the successful development, execution, and sale of creative work."
>
> *—Richard H. Needham,*
> *former senior vice president,*
> *DDB Needham Worldwide*

## One-to-One Marketing

One statistic says that we have access to the same amount of information in one day that our parents had access to in one year. We are now are dealing with an entirely new consumer who is savvy, sophisticated, processes information at a much greater rate, and selects from a wide array of media, says Pam Keehn, an account manager at TBWA/ Chiat Day. As a result, the dynamics of the world of communication have changed immeasurably.

Martha Rogers and Don Peppers explore these changes in their new book, The One to One Future. "Mass media is melting down," they say.[1] There is just too much advertising out there for any of it to be effective, and too many advertising messages chasing a diminishing consumer attention span. As mass media is beginning to collapse, interactive media is taking its place and enabling one-to-one marketing, the new communication that is necessary to compete and survive in today's information age.

One-to-one marketing seeks to develop long-term relationships by initiating and maintaining a lifelong dialogue with individual customers. Traditional mass advertising will fade into the background as three new forms of interactive advertising begin to dominate the media:

• Invitational advertising: Successful advertisers will have to stop shouting at customers and instead offer polite invitations to initiate a discussion. In the interactive future, consumers will be able to set their interactive television with advanced approval or refusal for commercials.

environment, the competitive environment, the product strategy, and the proposition. Pam explains, "To put it simply: the planner is responsible for the consumer, the account person is responsible for the brand—what the product stands for and what the environment is. And the creatives are responsible for the execution."

The creative people use the brief to execute a series of ideas that are then presented to the client. The client critiques the concepts and the agency goes back to revise the work. During the revision stage, account managers begin the production process. They develop budgets and schedules for all the different media. They organize upcoming meetings. They constantly communicate with the client—day in and day out.

When an agency is not developing advertising for a certain product, it is always planning—looking at the competitive environment, judging the competition, and figuring out the best place for the product to go. Pam notes, "There's always a line extension, a new model that's next, something on the horizon that you're planning for the next round of advertising."

Many industry insiders believe that you have to start as a secretary to pay your dues in advertising. "I never subscribed to that and I didn't do it," says Pam. Pam used her undergraduate degree in quantitative psychology from UCLA to earn a job in research before making a lateral move into account management. With her specific coursework and specialized knowledge directly applicable to the research department, she was able to bypass a secretarial position. However, at TBWA/Chiat Day all the secretaries move up into different positions within one year. "I would strongly suggest shooting for the account coordinator position and settling for the secretary position as opposed to going for the latter. I often ask applicants why they are applying for the secretary position when they have the credentials to begin at a higher level," Pam adds. Based on her own experience, Pam does believe strongly in horizontal movement, and wonders why "a lot of people aren't willing to start in a lateral function. My counterpart started in media, and I think it helped me immeasurably to start in research. But if you know you only want to be in account management, then starting as a secretary is probably the best bet."

To move from traffic to account management is a little different, says Pam, because it doesn't have the same strategic implications. Although you get to know all the logistics of the process, you don't necessarily get to strategize about campaigns and learn the client-centered, brand-conscious mindset that an account manager has to have. You're learning the process, which is important, "but anybody can learn the process. In general I find that a media, research, or planning background is preferable."

Landing a job comes down to a matter of timing and the pool of talent that exists at the agency at a given time. Pam explains, "When someone begins as a secretary we tell them to expect to spend a year in that position. If an opening comes up in less than a year, they should be ready to jump on it and fight for it. No one is held to a specific timetable if they are talented. They could be out of that position in six months; then again, it could take a year and a half for something to open up."

At the same time, secretaries are no longer confined to administrative duties. This is partially because today's leaner and smarter agencies have to use every resource to its fullest ability. It's also a result of technology, which has eliminated much of the grunt work at the lower levels, freeing up more time for substantive work. "I answer my own phone, I have my own computer, I do my own correspondence, and we no longer maintain files. My 'secretary' is doing competitive analysis," Pam notes.

For Pam, looking at a resume is much like looking at advertising. "So much of advertising is personal taste, and that's where it becomes so subjective." In general, she looks for a well-designed resume that is interesting, visually pleasing, and well-written. "I don't go for the pink paper and the purple writing. That's not the way to stand out. A resume with a name at the top that's horsy and big with misaligned type reflects poorly on your own presentation. This is you on a piece of paper. For me the way to stand out is to be smart and tasteful. And tasteful is subjective. All of advertising is subjective so it's important to realize from the beginning that you're being judged subjectively."

Pam likes to see a balance between business, marketing, and entrepreneurial experience and a diverse, well-rounded life. "The perfect candidate has a mixture of business savvy and a personal *joie de vivre*." Interestingly, Pam asks people about what they did in high school. "Later on in life you have to do things because you have to get a job. People think you will never ask about high school activities, but what I find is that people in high school who were interested in government or the school newspaper or who did things because they wanted to are self-motivated people. And it's the self-motivated people who are most successful in advertising. I like to see that drive

- *Solicited advertising: There will be a burgeoning market for advertising-on-demand. Consumers will search out and look up advertising when they are thinking about buying something or want to compare prices, features, or services. In addition to classified ads and the Yellow Pages, the Internet is the fastest growing type of solicited advertising.*

- *Integral advertising: As consumers discard mainstream media, advertisers will include brand messages as integral parts of entertainment and information programs. Product placement in movies is already big business. In the future, there will be a blurring between publicity and advertising: See the movie, then buy the T-shirt, get a set of the characters, and converse with the stars at the endorser's web site.*

[1]Peppers, Don and Rogers, Martha, Ph.D., "Advertising in the One-to-One Future," *Info World (Online)*, February 12, 1996.

> ❝ Ideas come from everywhere. Some times the best ideas happen on a boat or in the shower. It's your life outside the agency that gives you your ideas."
>
> *–Nancy Rice,*
> *former senior vice president,*
> *group creative director,*
> *DDB Needham*

beyond what's required and I almost view internships as requirements. [However,] if I see someone with eight internships versus someone else who traveled around the world for a year, I go with person who loves life. And that's what you need in advertising, a passion for life."

You also need some of the critical attributes that Pam seeks in her employees. To be successful in advertising, Pam looks for an individual with these particular traits:

◎ *A connoisseur of great advertising. Someone with an appreciation of great advertising wants to be a part of creating effective advertising. You don't have to be a heavy TV watcher or reader but you have to understand the purpose of advertising, says Pam. Someone who doesn't know why they want to pursue advertising or is just here because it's fun does not have the commitment or the drive it takes to create great advertising.*

◎ *Intelligent and intuitive. Pam notes, "You have to get people from one place to another by listening to fifteen different comments, assessing the situation, and moving in a single direction to achieve a positive outcome." You need to be able to make the connection between different pieces of information and make the jump to the next level or the next belief system.*

◎ *Inventive and innovative. Account managers were once defined as the "suits," the rational, logical, logistical business people. "Now, I don't think you can be a traditional problem solver," says Pam. In today's leaner and meaner advertising environment, you have to be multidisciplined. "To be an account person now you need to be a creative thinker, a media strategist, a consumer advocate—you need to be all those things rolled into one."*

◎ *Inspirational. Although this is a quality you will develop along the way, you need an infectious desire to create great advertising and be able to bring out the best in each individual working with you on the team.*

◎ *A risk taker. To be empowered, you have to have the judgment to make the right decisions. You have to look at a solution, assess the benefits, and take the risk associated with making a decision. You have to*

be courageous and have conviction because you'll
constantly be standing up and fighting for your ideas.

◎ *Resilient. Ideas will be flying around, and people will
be shooting you down, and you can't fold in the face
of adversity. If somebody doesn't like an idea, you
have to be able to deal with constructive criticism,
pick yourself up, and move on to the next one.*

◎ *Likable. Believe it or not, this is a big part of being a
successful account manager. Work for a common
goal. Value other people's time. These characteristics
are key to success and often stem from just being a
pleasant person.*

Advertising is a cutting-edge field. It is impossible to succeed
in this industry without moving with the times. This entails
having an open mind and being interested in and accepting of
innovation. To work at an innovative agency like TBWA/Chiat
Day this attitude is essential.

As advertising messages launch into the virtual world of
cyberspace, advertising agencies are doing the same. TBWA/
Chiat Day leads the pack with its virtual office. With only two-
thirds of employees actually in the office at any given time, and
one-third of resources going unused, TBWA/Chiat Day had to
create a more efficient environment—the virtual office. Now,
TBWA/Chiat Day executives can check out a cellular phone and
computer, allowing them to communicate with colleagues and
clients from home, the office, the car, or the beach. This
agency of the future is about managing change and turning
information into ideas. Corporate ladders, organizational charts,
and departmental divisions are buried with obsolete reports in
old filing cabinets. The agency now maintains a constant flow
of people into open work areas, which stimulates interaction
and generates ideas. It has often been described as a daily
cocktail party. Without offices, cubicles, divisions, departments, or titles, the employees—like their work—are interactive, innovative, and dynamic.

With a networked laptop computer equipped with e-mail, fax
and scanning capacity, electronic calendar, and meeting
organizer, and cellular phones capable of call forwarding,
messaging, and conferencing, employees and their ideas are no
longer confined to the office. Creatives have always had a freer
atmosphere, and even planners might just sit outside and watch
people go by—now, this is an acceptable way for everyone to
work. This new setup has allowed the rest of the agency to
rethink the way they work and what work means—it no longer
means just "sitting at your desk." Pam notes, "Going virtual

makes you walk around all the time because you don't have a desk, and I believe one key to account management is constantly walking around and sticking your head in places and finding out what's going on." You can't hide behind your desk or retreat behind a closed door—you are constantly visible. As advertising itself is held to greater accountability, so too are the employees.

At the same time, the virtual office affords more flexibility. With two kids, Pam can run an errand or pick up her children, keeping her pager and cellular phone on all the while, so that she's reachable virtually twenty-four hours a day. This has added more balance to her life but it hasn't necessarily reduced the stress. "It's supposed to make you work less, but I think, in truth, though it enables you to make your own schedule, you probably end up working more."

# *Creative Department: What's the Big Idea?*

## JOAN WILDEMUTH, COPYWRITER
### Grey Advertising

The creative department has long been revered as the most exciting place to be in advertising. Is it "the most fun you can have with your clothes on," according to Jerry Della Femina?[1] Do creatives really hang out all day playing ping pong and eating munchies while they toss around ideas? "The atmosphere is a bit like the TV show *30-Something*," admits Joan, a copywriter at Grey Advertising. "But it's much less glamorous. Brilliant ideas don't come in the form of a 'Eureka!'"

Joan's first job was as an assistant at Ammirati & Puris, an agency currently in the spotlight for winning the $200 million Compaq Computer account. "I wasn't even in the creative department," she recalls, "and I hated every minute of it, but I learned a lot about the business." She spent just two months there before earning a slot in the training program at Lintas (now known as Ammirati Puris Lintas). "I just happened to stumble in there with my portfolio, they liked what they saw, and I was accepted into the program," says Joan. Easier said than done.

More typical is the secretary at Ammirati who spent two years working on his book before getting a job, and the proof-reader at Altschiller who spent three years putting his book together from scratch, Joan remembers.

Putting together a portfolio of sample advertisements, a "book," is the key to landing your first job. A book should have twelve to eighteen sample pieces, recommends Joan, consisting

[1]As quoted by Katz, Judith A., *The Ad Game*, Harper and Row, New York, NY, 1984, p.178.

## What Is Creativity?

*Is creativity some obscure, esoteric art form? "Not on your life," says Bob Kuperman, president and CEO of TBWA/Chiat Day, known for its cutting-edge creativity. "It's the most practical thing a businessman can employ. Creativity is the tool used to make advertising effective by making facts come alive in a fresh, memorable, and persuasive way." Simply put, creative advertising is good business, the goal of effective advertising. And what is effective advertising? Effective advertising achieves greater sales at less cost. MCI had $79 million in revenue when it hired Ally & Gargano in 1979; three and a half years later that figure stood at $1 billion. Now that's effective advertising.[1]*

*Creativity, the buzz word in this business for the last thirty years, has not only been used inaccurately, but irresponsibly. That's unfortunate, because when understood and properly practiced, creativity does result in greater sales more economically achieved. Properly practiced, creativity can make one ad do the work of ten. Properly practiced, creativity can lift your claims out of the swamp of sameness and make them accepted, believed, persuasive, urgent.*

*The real question is, if it makes so much sense, why isn't everyone doing it? Simply because it involves risk. And why is it so risky? Because there are no rules or formulas for successful creativity. Sure, some will tell you that having people in your ad will achieve greater readership or that a headline should be no longer than five words and that boldface caps are harder to read, but when it comes down to it, advertising is fundamentally about the art of persuasion, and no scientist can tell you how to create an idea or how to use your insight and imagination.*

of three or four campaigns of three print ads each as well as a few single ads. Some students are also filming their own commercials now, and "if you can do that, great, but you better start with a great idea before you do TV," she warns, "and a lot of times you'll be judged as a junior strictly on your print ads anyway. If you can write a real smart print campaign, you can easily transfer into TV. You don't have to know the ins and outs of writing for TV to get your first job."

Desktop publishing programs like Photoshop can help you polish your book and will certainly make you look more mature and professional, says Joan, but don't be afraid to paste and glue and draw, if need be, to get your idea across. One creative director once told Joan that he liked her work but was still seeing a lot of people, so if she had any big ideas in the next couple weeks to write them down and mail them in. In other words, a great idea is a great idea and it speaks for itself, even if it's on a napkin.

If a solid book is essential to landing that first job, how important is your resume? "A college degree demonstrates that you can

> **"You'd be surprised at how many famous advertising ideas first saw the light of day on a cocktail napkin. In fact, I'd say the cocktail napkin is one of the essential tools of the advertising business."**
>
> *–Ted Bell, former president and CEO, Leo Burnett Advertising*

read and write coherently, but it does not translate into the ability to think strategically and creatively. A resume is virtually meaningless, and if you have a really fantastic book, I don't think you even need a college degree," Joan asserts.

But no matter how great your book and your resume are, you have to feel a sincere passion for the business, and you must have patience and persistence. You can't get discouraged even though you feel like giving up, even if it takes years to get that first break.

> **"I wrote thirty-seven headlines for Sears Roebuck, and I think I got three that I thought were good enough to submit to other people for their comment."**
>
> *–David Ogilvy*

"You'll throw yourself into your ideas and people will shoot you down again and again, but you have to realize that's part of the job. Your work will get rejected over and over. It's crushing, and you've got to be thick-skinned and resilient to survive. You'll have eight ideas and someone will kill seven and you've got to think that you didn't have seven bad ideas, you had one great one," Joan advises.

Once you have your book together, the next step is to call around and "beg people to sit and talk with you and allow you to show them your stuff in an informational interview, and I'm sure at first they'll hate it," Joan says matter-of-factly. This is where an internship can get you started. "It's extremely valuable to intern in the city where you are planning to work, because finding a job is all about talking to people and getting to know people in the business." Prospective copywriters who didn't necessarily have contacts in the business have used all sorts of gags to get attention, from the resume in a pizza box promising to "deliver the finest ideas," to the ads in a shoe, trying to "get a foot in the door." Joan warns that if you use this tactic you have to be certain that you come up with something clever and witty to grab someone's attention and make an impression, otherwise your attempt will backfire.

However you get in the door, expect to start at the bottom. "As a copywriter I think it's invaluable to start off as a secretary or "assistant" in the creative department," recommends Joan. Spend some time learning from other people in the department who can help you revise your work, and use them to build a network of people in the field. But be wary of taking an assistant position in another department, especially if the agency is a large one. "At Grey, a job in the media department would not help you because the divisions are very separate. At a smaller shop, that might not be the case—account, media, and creative people might be mixed up on the same floor. You want to make sure you have immediate access to other creatives to help you with your book," she says. At the same time, if you want to get a job with a particular agency because you love their work, take any job just to get your foot in the door, Joan recommends. Cliff Freeman, a Saatchi & Saatchi subsidiary, for example, is one hot shop where everybody is dying to work, and if you're really determined to work there, "by all means, take a job sweeping floors or delivering mail just to get in," says Joan. The field is flooded with young people willing to work for practically nothing—a typical junior salary is in the low twenties at a large agency, but Joan recalls a friend accepting a small agency's offer of $17,000 several years ago.

Joan worked at Lintas for a year and a half until they lost several accounts, and she was one of many laid off. She then spent the next several years jumping from Altschiller Reitzfeld to Wunderman, and ended up at Grey, where she's been a copywriter for two years. Each agency has its own style, she observes. Grey is very corporate and the account people run

Consumers are bombarded with more than 1,500 advertising messages a day, all seeking to be original and effective. How can you break out of the clutter? All great advertising has one thing in common, says Kuperman. "It's always preceded by a meeting in which someone says, 'Are you crazy? The client's never going to buy this!' People are afraid of risk, they're afraid of being different. Afraid of losing an account and losing their jobs."

"But what we miss is that it's in that exact place (the new, the untried) that the big rewards lie...Don't copy the style of great creative advertising or of the agency it came from. We have nothing to offer but used ideas," says Kuperman. "You have your own style, your own way of thinking. Take the risk of being yourself."

Bill Bernbach, one of the founders of Doyle Dane Bernbach (now DDB Needham), once said, "To keep your ads fresh, you've got to keep yourself fresh. Live in the current idiom and you will create in it. If you follow and enjoy and are excited by the new trails in art, in writing, in industry, in personal relationships. . .whatever you do will naturally be of today." Kuperman agrees: "Study advertising and you will not produce great advertising. Study life and you will."[2]

[1] Katz, Judith A., *The Ad Game*, Harper and Row, New York, NY, 1984, p.111.

[2] Kuperman, Rob, "Safe Advertising is the Riskiest Advertising," TBWA/Chiat Day online, 1997.

the show. They are viewed as having more power and their word is often final. At Altschiller, the creative director owned the agency so the creatives ruled. "I loved working at the smaller shops. At the larger agencies you tend to be removed from the process. I don't know any of the media people; I'm on the 10th floor and the account people are in a different section on the 23rd floor— they might as well be in a separate building. A larger agency is also much more political—you're trying to impress certain people rather than just doing your job well, and there is constant competition."

> " Please don't tell my mother that I am in advertising. She thinks I play piano in a brothel."
>
> –Jacques Seguela, creative head, Roux, Seguela, Cayzac and Goudard

Junior copywriters essentially do the same work as senior copywriters, the only difference being that they are not as skilled in the ability to develop and sell their ideas, and they'll spend more time doing so. Joan recalls working quite a few eighty-hour weeks at Lintas. "During your first year you want to impress everybody with your ambition and prove yourself, but you can be making $20,000 and doing the same work as someone earning $200,000." Most agencies will put four or five different teams of writers and art directors on an assignment and choose the best idea. Joan recalls that her first project was working on a television spot; she didn't get it produced, but notes that whether you're a junior or senior writer, you'll be given the same opportunities. Junior copywriters should expect to work on lots of radio spots, because the work is considered unglamorous and it's also easy to train someone to write radio copy.

The ability to sell your ideas is another important and often unrecognized skill that is a necessity for successful copywriters, but one that doesn't necessarily come naturally. "It's really frustrating to work so hard on a campaign and not be able to sell your boss or the client on your brilliant idea because they are convinced they want 25 seconds of the 30-second spot to focus on the product," says Joan. "I didn't realize I had to be a salesperson, too. You have to be able to sell your work to both the agency and the client. That brilliant idea is useless if you can't convince the client of why it's brilliant and how it's going to sell their product." This is where having a true passion for the business can help you succeed.

To be successful, you need to have an intense belief in your work, agrees Amil Gargano, cofounder of the former Ally & Gargano, which launched Volvo's success back in the early 1960s. The ability to sell your ideas is another important—and often unrecognized—skill that is a necessity for successful copywriters, as well as extensive knowledge about the client, product, and marketplace. "Conviction makes good work. It's the same with any kind of communication activity. If you believe something, you can go out there and convince others."[2]

Some days copywriters generate ideas for new campaigns, known as concepting, and other days they edit or rewrite copy or present their work to the creative heads, account team, or the client. "Every day there is a new problem to solve, and there is a lot of variety in the work," says Joan. "One day I have an assignment to sell wood glue to 55-year old home contractors. The next day I'm pushing lite yogurt to fat ladies in Cincinnati." But how can someone understand such radically different markets? Copywriters need to obsessively observe the world around them—from culture to current events. Read newspapers and magazines, go to movies, watch TV, and surf the Net—all with a critical eye, recommends Joan. "It can only help to have a well-rounded view of the world."

> "The art of advertising is getting a message into the heads of the most people at the lowest possible cost...what else is this business all about?"
>
> –*Rosser Reeves,*
> *(the former) Ted Bates & Co.*

In the same vein, the general consensus is that copywriters should have a broad liberal arts education rather than an advertising degree. Advertising, as an industry, is a multidisciplinary mélange of a wide range of studies, from literature and art to sociology and psychology. Joan went to the University of Oregon and got her bachelor's degree in journalism with a minor in economics. She took some general classes in media, account management, copywriting, and a couple of design courses. "I don't really know what an advertising degree does for you. You can spend two years at the School of Visual Arts taking classes on concepting and working on your portfolio. You learn how to write but not what to write about." In the real world it does take a long time to put together your first book, but with a more eclectic background you have a broader basis from which to generate that big idea.

This is a very exciting time to be a copywriter because technology has unleashed exciting creative possibilities—anything you can imagine you can now visualize, communicate, and produce with advanced computer applications. Technology has also made the process seamless, speeding up the creative process because "you can see your ideas right away and are able to play with them and manipulate them in a much more flexible way," says Joan. Computer technology has also

---

[2] Ibid.

overhauled the art director's job. Art directors now generate their own type and final high-resolution graphics, saving the time and expense of using typesetters and photo houses; artists produce finished "comps" quickly and in final form for clients' review; slides, color comps, and animatics have almost completely replaced traditional methods of presentation. Technology has also changed the relationship between writer and art director, blurring the lines between their jobs since both are capable of working both visually and verbally.

Technology is revolutionizing the process, but how is it changing the product? The new rule is that there are no rules. Steadfast guidelines regarding design and layout are now relics of the past as type becomes image and image type. Product shots, logos, headlines, and taglines dance unpredictably around the page—if they exist at all—and typical, comfortable visual balance is often absent. As visual and conceptual forms evolve, so does the language of advertising. Once there was a discernible wall between the product and consumer, medium and message. Now that new media venues afford one-to-one interactivity, the medium is the message, and the message is more personal. Advertising no longer consists of overblown claims, half-truths, or traditional jargon. The art of convincing has been replaced by the art of conversing—simply, honestly, and often self-consciously to a generation of savvy, sophisticated, and cynical consumers.[3]

[3]"Thoughts About the Future of Advertising,"Department of Advertising, The University of Texas at Austin, Dec. 1995.

# *Media Department: No Longer the Industry's Stepchild*

## SANJAY PRADHAN, VP OPERATIONS
### Sillery Mayer & Partners

Suddenly, media has become the most dynamic field in advertising. What will be the next evolution in interactive communication? With the combination of the explosion of media—from
cable and satellite television to the Internet—and the precise
targeting capabilities of new technologies, marketers are
depending on strategic media guidance for their businesses.
Media professionals are redefining who their audience is, what
they're doing, and when and how to reach them. A career in
media offers more opportunity, challenge, and fun than ever
before.

In 1988 Sanjay Pradhan took his first job as a media assistant,
answering phones and ordering lunches. Over the next seven
years he rose to become media planning supervisor, handling a
multi-million dollar retail account.

Armed with an undergraduate degree in mass communications
from St. Bonaventure in 1986, Sanjay went on to study communications theory at Syracuse University and received a master's
degree in advertising. He then moved to Boston to look for
work. But as an aspiring copywriter he didn't have much to
show except a collegiate portfolio and was disheartened that he
couldn't find a job.

At a meeting at the Boston Ad Club he met a copywriter who
told him about an opening in a small media shop. Six months
later Sanjay had his first job as a media assistant. "I still wanted

## Hot Trends In Media

to move into creative," Sanjay recalls, "but I figured, 'Hey, any experience is good experience at this point.'" The company was strictly a media shop, specializing in buying local radio and TV. "They call it media assistant, but it was really administrative and clerical. I answered the phones. I ordered food." And how much did he make? "The guy said, 'How much do you want' and I said, '$16,000.' He said, 'You won't survive. I'll give you $16,500.'"

After eight months as a media assistant he decided to move on. "I learned what I could, but I couldn't really learn very much because I was too busy taking messages and typing memos. I learned how account reps work and how local broadcast works. I didn't understand the details, but I learned the peripherals."

Packing up his car again, Sanjay moved to New York. His first stop was a personnel agency in midtown. He remembers, "They made me type, so I typed along with everyone else." If you are willing to take a clerical job as a media assistant, a personnel agency can get you in the door. But remember that only you can move yourself out of a clerical position. If you take one, he cautions, draw a line in the sand and tell yourself 'I expect to be here by this time and want to be given these opportunities.'

Sanjay then saw an ad for a barter media house, which pitches all sorts of companies with surplus goods and trades media time for their products. He got the job, but didn't know anything about barter. "I learned more about it as I went along and realized it wasn't my style. I learned what I could but found it incredibly dull. So I spent my time teaching myself about media. I read *Media Planning: A Practical Guide* by Jim Sermanek, probably the best book ever written on media—it's a great practical handbook."

Three months later Sanjay saw an ad in *Adweek* for an assistant media planner at Dewitt Media, a media-buying company whose clients include BMW and the Discovery Channel. "They gave me the same salary I was making, which was about $21,000. They offered me $18,000 and I said $21,000. I learned the art of negotiation right there. Salaries haven't changed much over the years. They'll offer you peanuts, but always ask for more," Sanjay advises. Average starting salary today is still $18,000 or $20,000. If they offer you $16,000, ask for $19,000. Three thousand dollars is nothing for a large corporation, he advises.

"The agency had a really phenomenal bunch of young ambitious people and we all taught each other," Sanjay recalls. "This was the real thing. This was where I learned what planning was all about." And during this process, the aspiring copywriter learned something new about himself. "I found out that I am a numerical person. Reading all the statistics came so naturally to me. I had never done a spreadsheet before and when I did, I realized that this is exactly the way my mind thinks. All this time I thought I wanted to work with words, only to find that I have a penchant for numbers."

The "real thing" also included working with tools such as Simmons Market Research and MRI. These two major suppliers provide syndicated research detailing demographic marketing information on people who consume media. The data are coded and can be cross-tabulated to combine different variables to provide a picture of the target audience and determine how to reach them. For example, what type of magazines do thirty-year-old men who own guns and eat Snickers bars read?

Planners are strategists, working in partnership with the client and the agency's account manager and creative group to formulate the marketing and advertising plan. They identify and characterize the target audience, recommend which media vehicles will best reach them, and consult on what forms of creative advertisements are best suited for those media. Sanjay chose planning because "you have to understand the dynamics of buying plus you have to understand media consumption in the United States. There's much more psychology and analysis involved."

Media buyers are experts in buying the media space in which the advertising will run, including network television and radio, spot (local) television and radio, print (newspapers and magazines), and outdoor (billboards, phone kiosks, bus cards, etc.). Buyers consider each medium's popularity with specific targets and competitive marketers to help them negotiate the best media position for the best price.

Sanjay spent three and a half years at Dewitt Media and credits the firm for teaching him everything he knows. During that time he jumped from assistant planner to media planner to senior planner. "This was the core of my learning experience. I didn't have an overall objective of where I was going, but all I knew was I had to keep learning. The more I knew, the more powerful I could be in the business."

How do you know if media is right for you? Sanjay explains, "I think when you're young you really don't know what you're good at yet.

- The blurring of advertising and editorial will continue. Infomercials (the first truly interactive medium) are making their way onto the World Wide Web. TV infomercials brought in $241 million in media in 1996, a 55 percent increase over 1995. Interactive television will offer new opportunities such as commercials targeted to individual households and virtual shopping.

- Career opportunities in media will extend beyond traditional advertising agencies and media shops. Online media planning is becoming a hybrid business as new companies form to handle media accounts, billing hundreds of millions of dollars.

- As new media develop, new media "people counters" will also be needed to track the effectiveness of advertising and provide quantifiable information for media planning. Familiar companies such as Neilson and Arbitron are entering this field, as are new companies like NetCount.

- Media planners are becoming marketers— rather than just number crunchers—in charge of new media efforts. "New media is not about technology," says Nicolas Kojey-Strauss, senior account planner/new-media strategist at Merkley Newman Harty, a New York-based ad agency. It's about developing new ways for brands to communicate with customers in a two-way, interactive relationship.

> "When you get your first job in the business, don't be concerned with salary because you're really continuing your education."
>
> —Lee Clow, chairman, chief creative officer, TBWA/Chiat Day

Most people go into media by default—you can't get into creative and you'll do anything to get into the business because it's so glamorous. Media has always been considered the step-child of the industry." But not so anymore. Media specialists are now in the hot seat in this age of information technology and interactivity. "We're a country that's obsessed with media. Pursue media if you like sociology, if you like analyzing how American society consumes media, and if you are interested in understanding consumer behavior."

You need to have solid arithmetic skills—but you don't have to be Sir Isaac Newton. You also need to know some kind of word processing and spreadsheet programs. Even though software will perform calculations for you, you still need to comprehend math and percentages to manipulate the data. The most relevant skill you need is solid, clear communication. There is a concise, logical way of writing, and you must be able to relate information clearly and succinctly to a client who's too busy to read.

Keep abreast of trends and developments in new media. Coming into the business with knowledge of the Internet and emerging electronic technologies is a nice shiny bonus for a newcomer and can make you stand out in the crowd. Almost every major agency has an interactive media division and experience in this area can only make you more marketable and valuable.

According to Sanjay, assistant planning and assistant buying are nearly the same position when you start out. You have to understand the core of what rating points are (what percent of the population viewed a given medium at a given time) and what markets are (specific geographic areas designated according to television broadcasting coverage). You spend hours checking sheets and sheets of dull-looking computer generated numbers. You also may end up doing data entry, listing markets all day long. You will perform post-buy analyses—after a buy, the planner files a report documenting that the advertising actually ran and estimates the size of the audience. Assistants will also begin to summarize buys and start looking at research numbers as a preliminary form of planning. And, most likely, an assistant will be a gopher for a media supervisor.

The work may seem monotonous and tedious and "you'll think, 'what a stupid job this is,'" Sanjay remembers. "During my first years I worked 60 hours a week," he says without hesitation. "Easily 60 hours, sometimes more including the weekends. I was stressed out and anxious, but it was worth it. There was so much grunt work to do, but you've got to get the grunt work done before you're going to learn. And you always have to be eager to learn. Know that the first several years are going to stink, but there is light at the end of the tunnel."

During your first year you will learn how to take a glut of information, analyze it, and summarize it into a one- or two-page memo. Learn how to summarize and use bullets effectively. Clients don't have the time or the expertise to interpret numbers, and it will be up to you to analyze and translate data into simple language.

Proficiency with spreadsheets is essential. Agencies have planning and buying software that they customize to meet their own needs. Most are based on Excel, so if you understand that program, you'll be a step ahead. "Everything in media is based on spreadsheets," says Sanjay. "If you can understand baseball stats, you can easily grasp media stats." You will also need to develop good organizational skills, which you'll use throughout your career.

Sanjay's career got off the ground with a contact at the Boston Ad Club. And although he's had good luck with newspaper ads, Sanjay is the first to admit that networking is the best strategy. "Ain't no substitute for networking," he says. "Always keep building your own little database."

Organizing an informational interview is as easy as saying to someone, "Hey, I want to learn more about what you do." "People love being treated like an authority. Flatter them and they'll ramble on. When they drop a few names you scoop them right up. Just go in there and pick their brains," recommends Sanjay. "You can't lose. Go in to learn. And at the end ask, "How would you recommend I break into this field? Are there any people you could put me in touch with?"

Such sessions should allow you to come out with a handful of names, or the realization that you want to stay the hell away from this field! "Networking will give you the best shot at finding a job," says Sanjay. "Because everybody wants to help a kid out and everybody sees themselves in that person."

The people you want to meet are the media supervisors and their superiors. Sanjay ridicules the concept of human resources. "They have no idea what's going on in the media department and what its needs are. They don't know anything—they are administrative people who keep a stash of resumes filed away."

How do you get the attention of the people with the hiring power? Be genuine and friendly and ask if they have a moment for you, Sanjay says. Forget about unnecessary formality and the color of your resume paper. Be genuine, warm, and enthusiastic. Be candid—I want to learn, here I am. There is no substitute for honesty and enthusiasm.

Interning can help give you an edge in finding your first job. While working on his Master's degree, Sanjay interned with a small creative agency. "I was bored to tears there," he remembers. "They just had nothing for me to do." The most valuable intern experience is in a formal, structured program. It's got to be academic and practical and challenging. "A small agency may just use you as a free gopher," he warns.

"Though I was disheartened with my experience, the father of a friend of mine, a vice president at Xerox, said to me, "Kid, at your age, any experience is good experience." And I think he's right. Just understand business. Any kind of business experience makes good sense. Particularly seeing how merchandising works, how marketing works. Every kind of business experience is applicable."

Highlight anything in your resume that relates to business, both practical and academic experience. Take out the fluff—get rid of your summer lifeguarding and lawn-mowing jobs. Everybody sees through it as filler. Sanjay recommends using the interview as an opportunity to talk about what you're doing for self-improvement—how you're going about continuing your education now that you're out of school. (Maybe this is a good time to ask yourself, "What am I doing for self-improvement?" And if the answer is, "Nothing," perhaps you need to find something.) For example, "I took the Dale Carnegie course, and started my interview off with that," he says. "When I demonstrated that I took steps to improve myself, people got interested."

Have a certain pride in yourself and know that you have something to offer. It's a matter of comfortable confidence. "This is hard to develop when you're just out of school," remarks Sanjay, "and I've found a lot of kids transpose this into arrogance. I call the middle ground 'aggressive humility.' You're humble but you're aggressive at the same time. You have to be humble; you're gonna have to pay your dues and take your licks, but you're always pushing for a little more."

After you land that first job you will most likely find that your supervisor is generally only two years older than you and instead of understanding why a task was difficult to accomplish, he'll simply blame you for doing it wrong. It gets emotional. You will have a dull job that's very stressful at the same time.

The person right above you is going to stand on your head so he can stand up a little higher. At this point you've got to be politically savvy and go one rung above that person to your boss' supervisor to get the helicopter view. Ask yourself how your work, which may seem like drudgery, fits into the grand scheme. "Those who get the big picture faster are more successful," Sanjay says. "That's a fact. Always ask yourself 'What does this mean? Where am I going? What is my objective?'"

Sanjay recommends spending about six months as an assistant, two years as a planner and two years as a senior planner, depending on how much stimulation you're getting and how fast you're growing. Always have a grasp of what you're learning and what you need to learn. Always push, always look ahead. Ask for more—more money, more work, more responsibility.

Looking back, Sanjay recalls, "you're not always sure of yourself. You're always thinking 'What am I doing here?' and it seems like the crises never end. Success is a question of always wanting to learn more and having a thirst for knowledge, almost in an academic sense. It's not even a matter of ambition—the money and the promotions will come later. The more you learn the more marketable you are."

After several years at Dewitt Media, Sanjay heard about an opening through a woman at the spot-buying unit of Foote, Cone & Belding, a division of TWC North Communications. Knowing when to move on is just as important as knowing how to get a job, he says. "I hit a finite point at Dewitt and didn't think everyone was getting a fair opportunity to shine."

FCB had just won the $20 million A&P grocery account and Sanjay came in as the media planning supervisor. "I was 28 years old at the time and this position was a *huge* step. This was a big account with many markets across the eastern U.S., local cable, spot radio, spot TV, grand openings, and massive number crunching and analysis. I learned a lot about working with a client and how business runs."

There he developed a retail niche and built a very strong relationship with the client and the creative agency. He left FCB after two and a half years, feeling that his future was elsewhere. When the agency responsible for A&P's creative work heard that he'd quit, it made him an offer to become director of operations. He took the position and brought his media and strategic planning experience to the creative agency. "It's a small agency, and I'm wearing many hats. Now I'm learning how creative works and how money comes in and out of an agency. In another four years I'll stop and think to myself how I can take this to the next step."

Sanjay believes that a medium-sized organization is the best place to start out—in a small shop your responsibilities are too diverse, and in a large place you get lost. "And New York is the only place to be. I would say 70% of American advertising goes through New York. The up-and-coming advertising cities may be fine. But in New York you can lose a job one day and find another the next. And you can take this experience anywhere. After you've made it here, you are an aggressive person with a tough, thick skin. The people I've come in contact with who work out West just don't have the drive that you find here. They don't have New Yorkers' 'teeth' that can eat you alive. This is the most stimulating place to be in the business."

# *Planning Department: Psychoanalysis of the Consumer*

## PHILL BARUFKIN, ACCOUNT PLANNER
### Leo Burnett Company

When Phill graduated from college in 1990, after studying economics at the University of Connecticut, he was interested in business but unsure of how to apply his knowledge. So he spent a little more than a year working with a small marketing consulting firm that handled qualitative consumer-oriented research, such as focus groups. "This gave me the background that opened the door for me to advertising," he recalls. He first explored other options, including corporate work and research suppliers, but the moment he walked into an advertising agency he fell in love with the environment and the culture. But it was more than the often funky and informal nature of the business that caught his eye. "I love the creative nature of problem solving—the process of studying a problem before solving it. There's a lot of thinking and strategy in advertising. You get a chance to be creative and smart at the same time."

Phill networked his way to the now defunct Geer Dubois through a former colleague from consulting. When the company shut its doors after three months he moved to Ogilvy & Mather, where he spent three and half years as planning and research supervisor. From there he was recruited for a planning position at Leo Burnett Company, Chicago's largest advertising agency.

A few years ago the industry magazine, *Adweek,* wrote that account planning—a new advertising discipline that originated in England—had become extremely popular in the United

States, nearing the hysteria that struck when the Beatles made their first trip to America. Its influence may not be quite that exciting, but account planning is certainly transforming agencies that are looking for an edge in developing distinct creative solutions.

"Everybody has a different definition of what research and planning are," says Phill. "Research is a tool that planners use. In traditional research you're given a problem and you go out and study it. It may involve several methods: tracking studies follow the consumers' habits over a period of time; copy testing gauges the consumers' reaction to an advertisement; concept testing evaluates the consumers' response to product positioning. These types of studies are often added value—they are related to understanding the consumer and the nature of the marketplace, but indirectly related to the process of generating ideas." The goal of planning is essentially to use intimate knowledge about the consumer as a means to develop unique, relevant, and effective ads.

Just how planners go about discovering this intimate knowledge is a little harder to uncover. The process of account planning is far from a process, according to Michael Llewellyn-Williams, director of account planning at Ketchum in San Francisco. "The word 'process' for me implies a repetitive, carefully controlled, fairly linear chronology, a step-by-step algorithm with an a priori understanding of where the beginning is, roughly where the middle is going to come, and where the end predictably comes. It's easy to become so enamored of the process that you forget to rechallenge regularly the presumptions on which the process is based, particularly when the circumstances at hand cry out for thinking and acting outside the box." Planners constantly rechallenge conventional advertising and marketing wisdom, in search of a better way to analyze a problem and develop a solution, says Llewellyn-Williams.[1]

A traditional researcher might only want to know why a consumer drives a particular model of car. But a planner digs deeper, delving into how people feel about driving, transportation, "road rage," and other related issues. Planners rarely write precise reports quoting respondents; rather, they "search, and look, and dig, and ask, and listen, and roll up their sleeves, and bury themselves in data until they can propose their findings to the creative team as a simple, relevant, and unique piece of evidence," says Nina Milosevic, vice president and planning director at Foote, Cone & Belding in San Francisco.[2]

According to Phill, planning involves three skills: understanding consumers and what's going on in their lives; possessing an

---

[1] Llewellyn-Williams, Michael, "How American Clients View Account Planning, A Personal View," The Account Planning Group Online.

in-depth knowledge of the product, and knowing everything about your competition. "Planning is part of the whole creative process, without compromising the science of research. It's about living and breathing 'the consumer'—bringing the consumer to life." Planners look for the big idea inside the mind of the consumer. "I'm an actor every day, trying to get inside the head of the consumer to understand his thoughts and behavior," says Phill.

> "There is an inherent drama in every product. Our number one job is to dig for it and capitalize on it."
>
> —Leo Burnett, founder,
> Leo Burnett Company

He has found that one of the great things about planning is that you never really do anything twice—each day is new and different and there is no routine. You might work on positioning concepts, develop recommendations for conducting research, or pretest research concepts. As opposed to traditional researchers, planners are involved in a project on a continual and daily basis. "Ultimately, my job is to think strategically about a problem in such a way that it inspires the creatives to solve it. My goal is to utilize research to recognize insights." Milosevic agrees: "The planner is constantly looking for knowledge and the ways to connect many little facts to an insight, an insight that consists of inner motivations, symbols, images, and myths."

Planners are becoming increasingly popular in the industry, though planning is handled differently from agency to agency. Leo Burnett is traditionally a research company where people "think like planners, constantly trying to figure out consumers' habits and behaviors," notes Phill. There is a growing consensus that planners are valuable contributors to the advertising process. A lot of hot agencies now have a planning or planning-type of mentality or discipline, and almost every agency has some degree of planning in it, observes Phill.

But breaking into planning at an entry level is very difficult, and more so without any experience. "I was fortunate to have skills from another job

The planner's challenge is to understand the relationship between the consumer using the product and the product itself. As consumers become more savvy about the latest technological innovations, they also become more discriminating. At the same time, they may know they need the product but are unsure of exactly why. Combine this with the speed at which new products and technologies are emerging and it is no easy task to understand a consumer who is changing as quickly as the world in which the products and services are being introduced.

Successful planners must be able to "understand the industry, the products, and the marketplace, and "sustain the search for unexpected answers," according to Milosevic. "It is a combination of finding innovative ways of asking new questions and translating the raw data of people's responses into advertising judgments. More often than not it takes intuition and courage in order to identify the nugget, accept it, and present it to the client."

> "My technique is to saturate myself with knowledge of the product. I believe in good depth interviewing where I come realistically face to face with the people I am trying to sell."
>
> —Leo Burnett, founder,
> Leo Burnett Company

[2] Milosevic L., Nina, "The Beatles vs. Planning," *PC World's Marketing Edge*, March/April 1995, as cited in The Account Planning Group Online.

which opened doors for me," says Phill, "and I would recommend seeking out jobs where you can acquire strong, general marketing experience that you can then sell to an advertising agency." A second way to break into the business is to be recruited from college. Leo Burnett Company hires people right out of school into its junior planning positions, and some large agencies are now recruiting on campuses, notes Phill, but this varies by agency. For instance, Ogilvy & Mather only hires people with some type of previous research experience and is not keen on training its employees.

Another way to break into the business is to have a very strong background in quantitative research, which involves mathematical and statistical applications. A survey is a simple example of a quantitative study that would measure, for instance, the percentage of people younger than thirty-five in the Midwest who "really like," "moderately like," or "dislike" the new, double chocolate Oreo cookie. Qualitative research, on the other hand, entails analyzing and interpreting consumers' thoughts and opinions. How do consumers feel about getting more chocolate in their cookie? Qualitative tools include interviews and focus groups, which are collective discussions with groups of consumers, as well as field studies in which researchers observe shopping habits or visit consumers in their homes to watch them use a product. (One agency with a plumbing fixture client even videotapes people's showering habits!) Ultimately, to be a planner you have to have well-rounded skills—you must have an understanding of both qualitative and quantitative research, you have to know how to use primary information, and where to get secondary information. It's also important to be able to synthesize information from multiple sources and identify patterns and trends.

Research and planning cover a broad range of interests and disciplines and you should be both a left-brained and right-brained person—able to simultaneously solve problems and be creative, advises Phill. Agencies are now looking for employees with diversity. If you want to be a planner, you should understand how to solve problems and love to go out and study different issues. Planners, by nature, are observers—they look around and constantly try to understand the world around them. It helps if you have a strong background in sociology, psychology, or human behavior, and a strong understanding of marketing won't hurt either, recommends Phill.

You don't have to have an exceptional academic record, but it's important to demonstrate a passion in a particular area of interest, whether it's a particular interest in life or in school. Anything that you are interested in and knowledgeable about can relate to and add to the value of advertising in some way, Phill believes. Showing that you are passionate about something, be it sports or music or art, demonstrates that you can apply that same passion to advertising. And although those interests may not form a clear linear connection, there is sure to be something that you can extrapolate from your experience and interest in life that relates to advertising.

Computer skills are essential for an entry-level job, particularly basic word processing. You also need to know how to use some type of graphics package like Powerpoint, and know how to use it well. "I see a lot of people who work underneath me who think they have an understanding of a program, but when it comes to putting together a presentation quickly, they don't know how to create charts and graphs and integrate spreadsheets." Computer skills will become even more critical not just for analyzing data, but for presenting it, agrees Jim Spaeth, president of the Advertising Research Foundation. Interesting findings are lost in a poor presentation, and data must be communicated in a way that is both intelligible and interesting.

*Hyperstudio*

Although it is not crucial for entry-level employees to have electronic research skills or Internet experience, you must be able to search for information when you're given a specific task or problem. Knowing how to use electronic resources can only help and has made my job easier, says Phill. "I used to spend more time with magazines and newspapers that my customers read—those who are part of my business, and those who I'm targeting. Which magazines do they read (and, more importantly, why are they reading them, what are they learning from them, and how is it influencing their lives), which web sites do they visit, and what are they saying in newsgroups? You learn a lot about people that way—that's how they get information that shapes their lives and culture. The Internet puts information at your fingertips to help put together a portrait of consumers' lives. It has helped me by cutting down the time I spend collecting, organizing, and reading material. There are also syndicated services that you can purchase that download articles and other information that can help you solve another piece of the puzzle in understanding the consumer."

Online research is a new frontier for advertising agencies, and Leo Burnett Company is exploring the possibilities of electronic studies. "You can have online focus groups, discussion groups, and tracking studies in which you can actually download the creative and the advertising for people to look at—this makes your traditional phone survey more dimensional so you can study the issues more effectively. I think this is only going to become more prevalent as people become more comfortable with technology," says Phill. Traditionally, the agent and client would have to travel to the focus group location, usually in several cities around the country. Now, focus groups are being conducted online; the agency in Chicago and the client in New York can "attend" a focus group in Los Angeles without ever leaving their offices. Today there is the perception that things are changing so rapidly that there is a need for immediate information. Researchers are also starting to talk about getting real time feedback from consumers, as opposed to planning a study for several months, carrying it out, analyzing it, and reporting the data, a process that can take close to a year.

During your first year it's essential that you learn how to think for yourself, and you should be doing much more than just "screeners" (crunching numbers on a computer screen), warns Phill. A junior planner reports directly to a planning supervisor and will take on the following responsibilities: compiling data from secondary resources, tracking the progress of research projects, and assisting in the development of primary research.

To be valuable, it's necessary to learn about the consumer as well as categories and brands so that you will have a better understanding of the product or service you're working with. You'll learn how to go out and get information quickly and turn it around, but you want to get beyond just executing assignments and learn how to think and solve problems creatively. This doesn't happen overnight. Expect to spend anywhere from two to five years as a junior planner before moving up, but that doesn't mean you won't get raises or promotions or increased responsibility within that position. Work hours during your first year vary from agency to agency, though you can generally expect to be living at the office. "I basically slept at Geer Dubois. The business we were working on was exhausting but satisfying," Phill recalls. But there is a light at the end of the tunnel—as your position increases, your hours will generally decrease.

There are three fundamental skills that a successful planner needs, according to Jim Spaeth. In the "olden days" researchers collected data, looked at the numbers, assessed numerical differences, and tried to produce statistically significant results. Today, as technology allows us to collect more and more information, planners must be able to analyze data. Researchers are using highly advanced statistical applications to draw out more meaningful information using analytical techniques such as modeling, conjoint analysis, discrete choice models, and consumer preference models. On the frontier are methods such as data mining and neural networks, techniques that border on artificial intelligence. The ability to integrate information is a key factor in planning—balancing the agency and client reports, qualitative and quantitative studies, and identifying patterns and connections. Equally important is the ability to discriminate—in this age of information overload with databases galore, it's crucial to be able to assess the source of information, understand it and its applications, and use it appropriately.

The ability to think independently and creatively is another critical part of research. It's guaranteed that the problem you're studying has already been studied to death by your competition, says Phill. Planners are not looking for what the majority think is the right answer. They're looking to shake things up by exploring new ways to solve problems and uncover that golden opportunity that maybe only one in a hundred people would think of, he says. However, the process is a Catch-22 because when you're dealing with multibillion dollar corporations, they need numbers and data and statistically significant results to support their decisions usually not conducive to ceativity.

> " My ideas about what constitutes good copy, almost all of them derive from research. Advertising people who ignore research are as dangerous as generals who ignore decode of enemy signals."
>
> *—David Ogilvy, founder, Ogilvy & Mather*

Having worked in several companies and two very different cities, Phill is intimately aware of how corporate culture varies from company to company. "I loved Geer Dubois' small, close-knit group of people, even though the work was chaotic and hectic," he remembers. Leo Burnett is a family-oriented environment, and they strive for more of a balance. "The company wants people to have a career as well as a life outside of work," says Phill. "There are definitely long days here, but not like in New York. It's also a very informal environment where people wear jeans and sneakers. People respect the company, and even though they work hard, you have the sense that they're having fun. It's all about loyalty—Burnett wants people to stay here forever. It's one of the reasons why they've been voted one of the top hundred companies to work for over the past nine years or so."

However, about ninety percent of advertising is still done out of New York City, making it more competitive and difficult to break into the business. "For an entry-level person, my guess is that it would be easier to get a job by starting elsewhere and then make the jump to New York. On the other hand, there are some benefits to starting out in New York. Once you've worked there, you have the credentials to work anywhere else. Because of the hectic pace of New York, both of the city and the advertising culture, you probably experience a lot more in your first few years than you would elsewhere. If you can get into a New York ad agency right after college, it would probably be the best place to start."

# *Traffic Department: Policing the Agency*

## SANDRA CLAUDIO, TRAFFIC MANAGER
### Adler Boschetto Peebles & Partners

The traffic department is the hub that connects the spokes of
the agency, ensuring that the advertising process runs smoothly
and on course. After the account group meets with the client to
develop an advertising campaign strategy, the account executives report to the traffic and production group, which work
hand in hand to estimate a budget and develop a schedule to
execute the campaign. The traffic department plans the flow of
work based on when ads are planned to run in newspapers and
magazines and develops a timetable so that each department
knows when its work is due to meet deadlines and closing
dates. Some traffic departments are autonomous with a specific
hierarchy of jobs. Other agencies integrate traffic personnel
into an account group and assign them to a particular piece of
business.

   If creatives are the thinkers and account managers are
affectionately known as the "suits," what are the traffic people?
"We are the pain in the butts," says Sandra. "Our job is to make
sure that everyone else does their job, whether we have to
plead, prod, coddle, or cajole them."

   Therefore, it's very important that you like the people you're
working with, and more importantly, that they like you.
Nobody wants their mother constantly looking over their
shoulder and telling them to do their homework, but that's
what you are. Now, if you can be a really fun, funky, cool

*Traffic Systems & Procedures, published by and available through the American Association of Advertising Agencies (4As), explains traffic responsibilities and types of traffic structures. Contact the 4As, based in New York, at 212/682-2500.*

mother—the kind of mother that every kid on the block wanted to have—then you've won half the battle.

Sandra looks for one thing in particular when interviewing an entry-level candidate for a traffic coordinator position: personality. And it's gotta shine. "I hired someone with 15 years' experience and then had to fire him because the guy was a dud. Nobody liked him, and being likable is a large part of being successful. You have to be able to communicate and get along with all different types of people from a variety of backgrounds. Not an easy task, but add to it the fact that you are the thorn in their side, and it becomes even harder. Surviving in traffic requires a tough balancing act between perseverance and patience. My motto is 'persistence...with a smile on your face,'" says Sandra. This is truly the department where you'll get to practice your people skills. You have to deal with each person's quirks and bad days and have an understanding of the character and temperament of each department as a whole. "Account people are bottom-liners. They want to know 'Are we on time, yes or no? Will the job get done or not?' Creatives are more laid back, carefree, and open to building a personal relationship. Having a good rapport with them is important when it comes time for you to be the bad guy. Don't even think about a job in traffic if you are shy or introverted. I barge into partners' offices and meetings if I have to. My job is on the line to get the job done," Sandra says matter-of-factly.

> "Be the kind of person others want to be around. I think that personality is as important as the work presented."
>
> *–Amil Gargano, co-founder, Ally & Gargano*

What else does Sandra look for in an employee? Demonstrate that you are deadline oriented and driven to achieve results, and use your resume to illustrate how you carry projects through to completion, she says. Show that you are well organized and can handle tasks in an orderly and systematic fashion. The ability to focus is also important—you should be able to prioritize while handling many projects at once. Although most people coming through the door have some marketing knowledge and a college degree, it's not essential—Sandra herself left school after two years. Computer skills are only necessary to use simple forms and type up schedules, but it is imperative to have top-notch computer skills if you plan to move into another department. And because you're not going to have the chance to hone those skills in the traffic department (if traffic is only a stepping stone to something else) it's best to be already proficient with word processing, spreadsheets, graphics, and presentation software when you come on board.

Traffic jobs, more so than any other department, are often handled by headhunters rather than the agency's personnel department; that's because traffic doesn't demand the same type of business background or specific skills required by other departments. How difficult is it to find a job? In New York, once you're in the business, it's relatively easy if you are laid off or are unhappy at your agency. Agencies are bought, sold, and merged all the time; accounts come and go; and the turnover rate in traffic is fairly high. In a city with approximately 850 ad agencies, you can lose a job one day and find a new one the next, says Sandra. She should know—she was hired twice by the same agency that fired her after losing a major piece of business and brought her back after several months. (Don't try this in Wyoming, though, home to just two ad agencies.)

Perhaps because of the high turnover or the high stress this job demands, a traffic job is well compensated. Entry-level jobs pay about $30,000, notes Sandra, substantially higher than any other department. That's with six months of experience; with two or three years under your belt, you can ask for $38,000–$39,000. The best way to get that initial experience is to intern or start out as an administrative assistant. Smart people are consistently promoted within twelve to eighteen months, says Sandra.

> **The 'helicopter quality': the ability to look at facts and problems from an overall viewpoint."**
>
> *—David Ogilvy, founder, Ogilvy & Mather*

Although traffic may not be one of the more glamorous fields, it is one of the best places to learn the business in an entry-level position. Traffic will give you an understanding of how each department functions, how each division works with the others, and how the agency functions as a whole. You gain a panoramic view of the entire agency's activities and interact with people in every department. As such, traffic people often move on to media, research, account management, and even client marketing. "I've trained three administrative assistants who then spent a year in traffic and were promoted to a position in account management. It's very easy to make a lateral move into another department."

"Working in traffic is not brain surgery, it's relatively easy. It's simply a matter of understanding the process and procedures, and that's something you can only accomplish through training." You will learn how to open up a job order, which initiates the process of a project; you will become familiar with the Standard Rate and Data Service (SRDS), which lists all publications—business and consumer—as well as costs for purchasing ads of particular sizes; you will learn how to create a production schedule; and you will learn how to route work and manage the interdepartmental work flow—from the proof-reader to the copywriter to the art director to account services to the client for approval, then back to production and out to printers and engravers.

Your hours will depend a lot on the type of account you are working on, "but generally you don't have to give your body and soul to the business. It is possible to also have a life." At the same time Sandra admits to working through lunch and staying until eight or nine every evening while working on the BMW account at Ammirati & Puris. Beware of airline accounts—they are notoriously difficult clients because destinations, prices, and special deals are always changing. Banks are also tough accounts because rates are always changing, says Sandra. An agency's culture also plays a role in how your job is defined. At Ammirati & Puris the traffic department is more structured and the processes are more rigid; at Adler, there is more freedom to define your own processes; you have more control over your job, and as a result, your hours.

Although technology has made other people's jobs easier, in a sense, it's made traffic harder, Sandra believes. Everything can now be done at the touch of a button, and work is constantly revised, edited, and changed. In the "old days," you couldn't change a hand-drawn storyboard without redoing it, but computers now enable instantaneous revisions at the last minute, and traffic is responsible for securing approval on every change, no matter how small. "I find this work very challenging, and I enjoy the high-pressured, frenzied pace, a pace that's becoming even more harried. Every day is new and different, and that's what keeps me in traffic. If you need routine, if you like to work behind a desk or sit in front a computer, this is not the job for you," Sandra concludes.

# New Business: The Cutting Edge of Change

**RICHARD MASTERSON, NEW BUSINESS DIRECTOR**
Ogilvy & Mather

Do you thrive under pressure and enjoy fast-paced work? Do you like to be on the cutting edge of economic change? If so, the new business department may be the place for you.

An agency's new business division supports senior management in competing for and winning new accounts for the agency. When a potential client contacts the agency, the new business department conducts secondary research to determine if the client is a worthwhile prospect. If the agency determines to pursue the prospect, the group is then responsible for assembling credentials information and arguments as to why the agency would be the best partner for the client.

The prospect may then ask for speculative work on its account, at which point the agency would be asked to solve a marketing problem, an organizational problem, and possibly even create new advertising. The new business group then collaborates with senior management to assemble a team with relevant experience. The group, comprised of members from planning and research, account management, creative, media, and possibly also direct response, public relations, and interactive marketing, works with the new business department to address the assignment and develop the campaign. New business is also responsible for the administration of new business projects, from managing the process and organizing meetings to designing the final presentation.

## Globalization

*"Globalization is the driving force in advertising, and it's fueled by technological development,"* says Richard Masterson, new business director at Ogilvy & Mather. *"Computer networks are shrinking the world dramatically, and businesses are seeking the most cost-effective means to manage their advertising and communications. You don't want to have four separate organizations in four regions of the world doing the same thing when you can send information around the world from one location. I envision that we will manage new business globally within five to ten years, with one larger department and a global satellite in each region."*

*As new technologies evolve, there are suddenly new agency searches for companies like Netscape. In New York alone, new media companies are a $2.8 billion industry, and there are more than 2,000 new companies, each looking to win an audience and establish a brand.[1]*

*Richard says, "We are completely technology-driven, and we're pretty much on the edge of what can be done with PCs. We do lots of desktop publishing and database work, and we interface with service bureaus and printing services. We are always on the Internet to gather information and we subscribe to electronic databases. It's critical to stay ahead of the curve to be competitive. We are constantly learning and upgrading our presentation capability, database research, international communication networks, and strategic applications."*

[1]Chen, David, "New-Media Industry Becoming Juggernaut," *The New York Times*, Oct. 23, 1997, p. B12.

So what does Richard Masterson and his team do on a day-to-day basis? "Research is the primary focus of our work. As part of the process of acquiring new clients, the new business department studies industries and specific companies and compiles prospect lists with relevant data. The department maintains a database of all the agency's case histories, past work, and knowledge of categories, and, like many worldwide agencies, we are attempting to compile a definitive master database to capture the agency's global experience."

The group also keeps databases of personnel, which categorize employees' relevant work history and detailed experience with other companies. In addition, new business conducts intra-agency research—in a worldwide agency there is diverse account experience in different places that is sometimes difficult to unearth, so the new business department is an expert in its own network. "We handle so many different businesses for so many different clients—our work is very dynamic because every month there are new campaigns breaking. We are constantly pulling relevant information, reconfiguring it, and shaping it into powerful arguments."

Some small agencies do have a new business director or a two-person department, and others may assign the responsibility to a senior account executive. But most large agencies have a dedicated new business group. "Due to this consulting trend, all the top agencies have new business groups since we have to answer extremely long and detailed questionnaires quite frequently, which requires quite a bit of work," notes Richard.

Agency reviews are driven by economic change, and "in new business you feel like you are constantly at the forefront of business developments. Advertising can be pretty exciting if you're lucky enough to be the creative director on Nike, but a lot of people are doing account management on toilet paper. There are a lot more of those jobs, and it becomes pretty repetitive when you're just making sure that ads run in the *Wichita Daily Journal*, for example. Once you have a strategic and creative direction, a lot of the work is day-to-day drudgery, whereas new business is always looking for new ideas, and we are always on the cutting edge of change."

New business is the place to learn about a variety of industries and explore new territory. But remember that prospective clients are scrutinizing the agency and subjecting it to a rigorous process of review, and the agency lives and dies on the success of its ability to win new accounts. The result is extremely urgent and intense work. "We get fairly unrealistic requests from clients for huge amounts of information and original thinking in a very compressed time frame, which can be as little as one week. As a result, we might end up working on a project nonstop, basically having no time to do anything else except sleep, sometimes not even that," Richard warns. "It's exciting and challenging to continually be at the heart of the action—we pursue a business intensely and we win or lose. But the phone can ring and suddenly you're working an eighty-hour week. The hours are uncontrolled, and if you can't work all night, this is not the job for you."

If it is the job for you, you'll start as a coordinator, a typical junior-level position. Coordinators are responsible for maintaining the agency print collection used for display during meetings, which requires a detailed understanding of the agency's work. Research is also an integral part of this position, using the library as well as online information. Creating presentations is another part of the job, and Richard expects a coordinator to be very active and creative in developing document presentations, particularly Powerpoint slides.

Coordinators do have administrative but not secretarial duties, the grunt work that "just has to get done." But entry-level jobs that have an administrative component shouldn't be sniffed at because with voice mail, e-mail, and a computer on the desk of every executive, there's more opportunity to become involved in substantive work. In the old days, administrative-level employees would have been photocopying, typing, and answering phones. "Today, a lot of that weight has been lifted," observes Richard. "With a powerful networked computer, there's an opportunity for you to find meaningful ways to contribute. In new business there is generally a lot more work than we can do, so this is a good job if you have a lot of initiative. You can be writing research reports pretty quickly and actually have a point of view on a category or an area of information. If you can use a computer to figure out how to help the business, you can get yourself promoted."

That's advice from the heart. Richard began at Ogilvy & Mather as an administrative assistant in account management and was hand-picked to join the new business department because he'd earned a reputation for his computer skills. He was then put in charge of creating presentations, and with his strong research and writing ability, he was promoted into more strategic work. Today, as a vice president, he advises the agency on how to approach a particular prospect and meets with clients to discuss agency credentials.

In addition, he is in charge of the department's staff. How can you get the attention of this high-pressured, high-powered executive? "Say something meaningful to me. Clip some articles from *Advertising Age*, *Adweek*, and the advertising columns in

> "I read *The New York Times* every morning...and I rip out ads that for one reason or another strike me as being effective communications. I have [a] file which is a bulging one—ads worth saving—which I've had for 25 years."
>
> —Leo Burnett, founder
> *Leo Burnett Company*

*The Wall Street Journal* and *The New York Times*. When you see an executive identified with a quote, that's a great opportunity to say, 'You said this and I think it's smart. I'd love to come speak to you.'

New business directors are sometimes harder to identify, so another tactic would be to make some substantive comments about something the agency president said that could then be passed along. If you write a letter that reads, 'I had a grade point average of 3.7 and was on the debate team so I think you'll really like my skills,' that's fine; but a better letter says, 'I see you recently won this account and you're doing a global organization around it utilizing new technologies, and I think that's fascinating because your creative works really well with your strategy...'"

In other words, new business directors are not spending their days thinking about great things they could do for young people who are pure potential; rather, they're busy and harried people who will respond to some genuine interest.

Once you've captured their attention, dazzle them with a resume that suggests that you could make their job easier. These days, when you can run a resume and cover letter off on your word processor, there's no reason not to have it be fairly specific and demonstrate that you understand who the agency is and what it does. "I look for a well-written, specific resume. I'm less interested when I receive something that looks like it was sent to 100 other agencies. Or something that says, 'I'm a fine person. Do you have a job for a fine person?' I want someone who actually has some ideas already."

Office work experience, in any capacity, is highly desirable—you should know what an office atmosphere is like and how an office functions. This is where an internship is invaluable. "Someone without an internship will always lose to someone with an internship, other things being equal," says Richard. But non-business related experience does count if you position it correctly. Waiter/waitress experience is a good skill to have, and one that Richard has drawn on personally. "At rush hour you have thirty people clamoring for attention and you have to stay calm and operate in an efficient manner under intense pressure. You take a bunch of orders and need to make one trip, rather than five, to the kitchen or the bar and back to the tables or you fall further and further behind. On the same note, this ability to 'multitask' is crucial in new business to successfully handle many demands in a compressed time frame. We might be designing one thing, researching another, and dealing with several people at once. You have to stay calm and handle one thing at a time and be strategic about the most efficient way to solve a problem instead of wasting steps."

When you are handling many tasks at once, there is no time for shabby computer skills. Richard warns, "Fast typing, a hundred words a minute, is critical. You're not going to be typing other people's material, but you have to be able to put together presentations and organize information quickly and efficiently. We would also love to see some advanced capabilities in the area of data or design, someone who can look at a problem and come up with solid strategies for putting data into the computer. That might be putting information into a spreadsheet instead of just a word processing document or organizing images in a design and layout that will be used again."

Your polished skills will pay off in new business, because although the hours can be strenuous, you will be well compensated. Entry-level employees generally earn overtime, and they can make "a ton of money," close to double their salary, Richard estimates. And there are other perks, as well. Large agencies pay for meals and transportation when you work late, and when there are presentations outside the agency the coordinator gets to travel.

In new business you also have the opportunity to interact with all the other departments, and it's a good launching pad to figure out if you want to work in account management, media, or research, and to make contacts that will allow you to make that transition. "Our group is small, so upward mobility within the department is limited. Expect to pay your dues for about two years—I know that seems like forever if you're twenty-two—but if you work hard and want to move into another department, I'd be happy to help," says Richard.

# PART TWO

## The Non-Traditional Agency

Technological and social changes have created new and explosive developments in the advertising industry, offering huge opportunities for those interested in a career in advertising. What are these new avenues? How do they differ from the traditional job? How can you begin a career in such an agency? Eight young professionals who have "made it" reveal the answers to these questions and tell their own stories of personal journeys to success.

# Ethnic Agencies: Streamlining Your Market

## JOHN STEERE, PRESIDENT
### Info Pacific Communications

How do you choose your shampoo? Do you need oily or dry formula? Do you want to detangle or defrizz? Add shine or volume? Moisture or protein? Think about how much time you spend debating in the shampoo aisle and how advertising affects your decision. Now imagine someone who has immigrated to this country trying to make the same choice between hundreds of unknown brands—in this case, shopping may be a very intimidating experience. "In fact, cultures like Vietnam have no advertising culture, so it's up to us to create one from ground zero," says John Steere, president of Info Pacific Communications, an agency that specializes in culturally specific advertising.

John, who is half Chinese, was born in Saigon and grew up in Pakistan and Taiwan before attending the University of Washington. After graduation he gave tours in China, worked for a venture capital company in Hong Kong, and ran a public relations agency in Taiwan. John then came to New York and spent a year as the general manager of a local agency with an Asian focus before starting his own company at the age of thirty.

John founded Info Pacific Communications to study how recent immigrants, particularly Asian Americans, make their purchases, and to create culturally sensitive advertising in their own native language. "While most Asian-Americans immigrants understand English, many still speak their native language at home. Will first- and second-generation Asians quickly

## Steere Report, "Memorable Blunders"

*Coca-Cola creates its Japanese commercials in Japan and hires Japanese actors, but the thinking behind the work is evidently American, says John Steere, president of Info Pacific Communications. One recent spot that aired in Japan depicts how the American mentality can be misinterpreted in the Japanese culture. The ad opens in an isolated roadside diner in the American Southwest. As Japanese teenagers walk hesitantly inside, the camera pans across a room full of typical American rednecks—burly, bearded, beer-bellied guys wearing cowboy boots and jeans. (Keep in mind that when the Japanese portray Americans in the media, they are generally made to appear much friendlier and kinder than Americans really are, though the Japanese people really see Americans as tough and dangerous.)*

*The Americans give the Japanese boys a cold stare as they approach the counter to buy something. Suddenly, one boy in a constructed Japanese accent says, "Coke, please." The men's stone faces suddenly burst into smile, there's broad laughter, back-slapping, a tagline, and logo—end of story. The lesson: "America is a melting pot nation of immigrants where you're only a stranger for a moment…and Coke is the bridge between strangers," says John, according to American interpretation.*

assimilate in America? And does traditional advertising, such as network television, reach this market? We believe there is still a need to talk to them in their own language because American advertising excludes them, makes them feel like they don't belong. Over half of Asian Americans are more likely to buy a product advertised in their own language."

This does not mean *translation*, which is considered a dirty word in the business. In any language advertising must be created from scratch. Pepsi learned its lesson when "Come Alive with the Pepsi Generation" was mistranslated into "Pepsi Brings Your Ancestors Back from the Dead." Creating original ads in consumers' native language avoids cultural and linguistic blunders and makes ethnic consumers feel like the advertiser is talking directly to them by relating to their personal experiences. For example, pronouns are completely avoided in the Japanese language; and the Japanese view conceit as completely undignified. Any ad that screams, "We're the best…" is completely off track, regardless of the rest of the message. Asian cultures are also averse to insulting a competitor, so something like the Pepsi/Coke challenge would never work in Japan. "Presentation, appearance, and context are extremely important, sometimes even more important than the actual factual content itself," notes John.

In addition to linguistic differences, there are a vast number of cultural differences in the ways Asian Americans manage their money and make purchase decisions. Vietnamese Americans, for example, adhere to the traditional model in which the man makes the decisions for large purchases, such as automobiles, electronic equipment, and financial services, and women are given a budget allocated to household expenses. So should ads targeted to the male Vietnamese audience only feature men? Absolutely not. The beautiful, young female models who appear in advertisements for the vast majority of products are appealing to consumers, regardless of who buys the products. "It's all about image," says John. "Associating your product or service with a beautiful young woman evokes freshness, allure, and modernity in this culture."[1] At the same time, image isn't everything, and Vietnamese expect you to educate them about a product. "They don't want to see catchy or humorous ads. They want the facts—what can you offer me and how much is it going to cost?"

On the other hand, effective advertising to Indian-Americans should focus on service. Labor is cheap in India, and many household chores are routinely performed by outside help.

---

1 Steere, John, "How Asian Americans Make Purchase Decisions," *Marketing News*, March 13, 1995.

Indians are accustomed to ordering a range of products over the phone for delivery. Therefore, products that promise to make life easier and more convenient are very appealing to this segment of the population.

These are complex issues to unearth, yet ethnic agencies have gotten a bum rap from general agencies who don't see African American, Hispanic, or Asian specialty shops in the same professional light. But this is quickly changing as these markets and corresponding advertising budgets are increasing. The Asian-American market is the fastest growing in the United States, doubling in number from 1980 to 1990 as a result of immigration. Fifteen years from now, 15 to 20 million Asians will spend an estimated $100 billion a year in the United States.[2] Ethnic agencies are stepping up to the challenge because mainstream agencies are ignoring this growing market.

"We maintain the same level of professionalism, offer the same kind of strategic thinking, and have the same dedication to client services as any traditional agency," John states.

Telecommunications, insurance, and financial industries are major players in ethnic marketing. These industries dedicate a substantial amount of their budgets to the effort. AT&T spends $20–$30 million per year on multicultural advertising, but "most ethnic ads target black and Hispanic [consumers] simply because of demographics. The focus is now shifting to Asians, who typically have a higher spending level, better education, and are more technologically savvy, making this a very attractive group of consumers. As a result, corporate America is beginning to take this market more seriously," observes John. MCI is the leader of the pack, targeting multicultural ads to nineteen different minority groups.

Info Pacific's clients include businesses particularly important to recent immigrants: MCI, Moneygram, and Fannie Mae, a company that helps recent immigrants purchase their first homes, are among the agency's roster. Clients come to an ethnic agency because they don't have the expertise needed to market their product effectively to groups not born in the United States. "There are not a lot of account managers who understand ethnic markets, so it's our job to educate the client."

The Info Pacific staff is comprised of recent Asian Pacific immigrants from Vietnam to Indonesia, Hong Kong to Taiwan, and they understand the mindset of the consumer because they have lived it.

"If you are a Hispanic who grew up in Miami, you can relate pretty closely to your culture, whereas the lives of American-

*But, in eastern Asia, where ancient rivalries have separated people for thousands of years, there is no equivalent of the American "melting pot" concept. This is most true in Japan, with its history of self-imposed isolation from the outside world. The Japanese interpretation of this commercial is that America is a scary place where you may find yourself stranded helplessly among dangerous, violent people who won't talk to you, and that even if they laugh, the intensity of their laughter mirrors their explosively aggressive impulses. Your only hope of survival is to know some secret code word, and even if you do crack the code, Americans will still laugh derisively at you but you'll escape harm.*

*Will Coke be recognized for its product? Or will its strategy that seeks to universalize American values in a country where that effort has been met with resistance for thousands of years backfire?[1]*

---

[1]Steere, John, "Memorable Blunders: The Pause That Turns You Into a Statistic," *The Steere Report*, Vol.1, No.3.

---

[2]Steere, John, "Exploding Asian-American Populations Still Elusive to Marketers," *The Steere Report*, Vol. 1, No.1.

born Asians are very different from the recent immigrants' experience. Therefore, we look for people who speak their native language, who were raised in traditional ethnic homes, and lived in or travel to their motherland—these are all important factors for our creative people. There are so many nuances to creating culturally sensitive work that it's essential to [completely understand] the culture in order to develop effective and appropriate ads." Nike found this out when it had to recall millions of its new Flame line because the graphic inadvertently resembled the symbol for Allah. Even draping a kimono left over right or right over left in an ad has a world of different connotations, says John.

> **"No matter how much money they give you, if you don't fit into the agency's culture it's not going to work out."**
>
> *—Steve Hayden, former chairman and chief creative officer, BBDO West*

"On the account services, media, and research side, I will go with an Asian American who has worked in a mainstream agency but wants to switch to the more cultural side, even if they haven't lived in their homeland. That shows me that they have an interest and desire to apply their skills to their culture." Account management skills are comparable in this industry: attention to detail, organization, communication, and generally servicing the client.

Account people become "market managers" at Info Pacific, specializing in one particular market. They need to understand census data and demographic information, comprehend media and markets, and be able to research information that is not immediately available. Status reports, timelines, and budgets are also an assistant account executive's responsibility.

> **"What you believe, if you believe in something deeply, and you know it, is going to come across even if you don't have the skill your competiton has. Now if you can combine skill with a deep belief, you're way ahead of the game."**
>
> *—Bill Bernbach*

Account and media positions are typical entry-level jobs and "we train a lot of people who just have a solid head on their shoulders," says John. "We also teach people the inner workings of production for a job in traffic. My business revolves around service and maintenance, and attention to detail is a primary focus for work in any department. I also really like to see young people with foresight and strategic planning skills who can go beyond just satisfying the client and are able to think ahead, point the client in a different direction, or introduce the client to something new. We want people who can be more of a tactical business partner rather than simply execute or produce the client's directives."

Info Pacific also has an interactive division and is the only agency that handles ethnic and multilingual web sites. Japan currently leads the world with 1.5 million Internet users, and Asian Americans make up three percent of web surfers—an impressive proportion in a country that accounts for only four percent of the world's population. Japan is followed by South Korea, Hong Kong, Malaysia, and Taiwan in the number of Internet users; Singapore has the highest level of Internet use per capita in all of Asia, where there is a computer in one out of every three homes.

Of the 2,000 plus sites related to Japan, about 400 feature businesses, accounting for approximately 20 percent of total Japanese sites. Other Asian countries like China and Vietnam also have a fair share of business-oriented web sites. This is an area that has explosive growth potential, and commercial sites are popping up, such as Asian Mall, ABC Flash, and Channel A, where Asian-owned companies are advertising their products online and facilitating interactive purchases. Info Pacific developed MCI's 'Hello India' site after finding a sizable Indian community on the web advising each other about the best-priced telecommunications company.

> "The people who will really make a name for themselves in the 1990s will be people who go beyond the page...people who see beyond the barriers, the visionaries."
>
> *–Susan Gillette, president,*
> *DDB Needham Chicago*

If you are interested in getting into ethnic advertising but don't have a specific cultural background or experience to bring to the agency, working on the interactive side is ideal because you can learn the ethnic business from the folks on the advertising side. HTML or programming skills will get you into this department, where you can then work with creative people from the general agency to incorporate cultural elements.

The future of ethnic advertising is full of opportunities for young people interested in joining the advertising industry. "Globalization is the major force shaping the industry," John asserts. "Technology enables you to develop advertising for any country anywhere in the world all in one locale. The budgets for large agencies, such as Saatchi in Hong Kong, are phenomenal, and profits all get put back into overhead. Scandinavian Airlines has a worldwide personnel in one location, develops a unified strategy, creates the ads, and distributes them to local account executives for media placement. This is the future of ethnic advertising," John emphasizes.

# *Healthcare Agencies: What's Your Specialty?*

## WENDI SHERMAN, ACCOUNT SUPERVISOR
### Cline, Davis & Mann

Wendi had no idea that medical advertising even existed while she attended college at the University of Gainesville. "When I graduated, I knew that I wanted to work in advertising, but I had never interned and that was a big mistake. I was the director of advertising for a student magazine, but I had no hands-on experience in an advertising agency."

She moved back to New York and made the rounds at the employment agencies, "but they only cared about my typing skills and I knew I would have to start at the bottom. I believed the same opportunity existed for me in either a medical or general agency, so I took a job with a medical agency because the salary was higher, " she recalls.

A medical advertising agency operates in much the same fashion as a general shop. The departments are organized in the same way and the agency conducts similar market research to develop a creative strategy. The main difference is the target audience—medical agencies advertise to physicians as well as directly to consumers (DTC). In fact, medical agencies now compete against general shops to win consumer business.

The medical advertising agency of record for a specific drug is essentially responsible for all aspects of marketing that drug, whether it's launching a new drug or a drug with a new indication, or relaunching a drug that has been on the market for several years. Medical agencies also handle promotional materials. In addition to advertising, they are responsible for direct marketing to physicians, informational brochures about drugs, reminders for medical offices, medical convention materials, patient and physician educational brochures and films, pharmacy promotional materials, and all of the materials that drug representatives use when they speak to physicians. In addition, medical agencies also promote their clients' drugs to the managed care industry.

More than 100 medical agencies (fifty of which are large) compete for accounts in the United States and almost every major agency has a healthcare division, including the following:

- ◎ *Omnicom Group: Cline, Davis & Mann; Harrison Star; Ketchum Healthcare Communications; KPR; Frank J. Corbett; Lyons Lavey Nickel Swift*

- ◎ *DMB&B: Medicus Group*

- ◎ *EURO RSCG: Robert A. Becker; Lally McFarland & Pantello*

- ◎ *Grey Advertising: Grey Healthcare Group*

- ◎ *Saatchi & Saatchi: Klemtner Advertising*

- ◎ *True North Communications: FCB Healthcare*

- ◎ *WPP Group: Commonhealth*

- ◎ *Young & Rubicam: Sudler & Hennessy*

Wendi started with Cline, Davis & Mann in 1991 as a receptionist, a good way to begin if you're unsure of how you can best contribute to the agency. "I was kind of creative and didn't know if I wanted to pursue art direction, and production also looked interesting. I was also interested in medical education, a whole other part of the business that involves running symposiums and conferences." But no matter where she was headed, she made sure she didn't stay in reception for long. "I went to all the department heads and asked them if they could give me extra work I could do in between answering the phone," she recalls. "It's really important to know what you want [or at least what you don't want] and be proactive."

It's also important to give yourself a goal and a deadline for a receptionist-type position, says Wendi. She also recommends that you ask specific questions about your job: Can I be promoted from this position? Who else has done so? How many people am I going to be working for? "Certain agencies don't promote internally. They may want a seasoned secretary and might not be interested in your career growth," she warns.

Although you definitely have to pay your dues, it may not take as long in a medical agency. Three months after she started at Cline, Davis & Mann—during the company Christmas party—Wendi approached an executive whose secretary had been promoted and asked for her job as the administrative assistant to the account services group. This aggressive, proactive approach paid off.

Wendi explained, "I worked for nine account people, from account executives to senior vice presidents, and typed up presentations (known as decks), trafficked material, assisted with research. Whatever was needed, I did, and I worked until seven or eight every evening. I also became very involved in coordinating new business pitches. This was a great place to be because I had contact with a lot of different departments and became intimately involved in the advertising process."

Other entry-level options at a medical agency include assistant positions in media and traffic, and a previous internship in a medical agency will certainly put you a step ahead. If you're interested in copywriting, make sure you really have a passion for science. "Don't even think about being a copywriter unless you are thrilled by science. You'll have to deal with a myriad of technical details and references; it's not an easy job. Art direction skills, though, are easily transferable." Being computer literate will help get you in the door, says Wendi. You should be adept with word processing as well as Excel, and it would definitely be advantageous to know Powerpoint. Experience in an office environment is highly preferable. You should also be proactive, a team player, and very bright (medical agencies *will* ask for your GPA). You also must have an openness to science. Not only is this a career in advertising, but "this is a career in healthcare and you should be aware of what this means," Wendi advises.

> "I have always tried to hire what J.P. Morgan called 'gentlemen with brains.' It doesn't necessarily mean a high I.Q. It means curiosity, common sense, wisdom, imagination, and literacy."
>
> *–David Ogilvy, founder, Ogilvy & Mather*

As a result of her hard work as an administrative assistant in account services, Wendi was promoted to assistant account executive about six months later. Her first project was on a piece of business that she had helped win for the agency. As an assistant account executive she handled weekly status reports, which track a project's schedule and billing, made sure jobs were trafficked throughout the agency, and communicated with the client about administrative needs. Though she did not have any involvement in determining the actual advertising, she was invited to attend all the meetings. "The advice I was always

*Last year, the top fifty pharmaceutical companies collectively generated $288 billion in worldwide healthcare revenue, an 11 percent increase over 1995, and boosted their sales force by 12.5 percent. 1996 was the best year ever for the U.S. pharmaceutical industry, and 1997 should be another banner year, according to Styli Engel, editor of Medical Advertising News. Look for the following trends to drive the industry's long-term growth and, in turn, increase the need for advertising professionals who specialize in medical products:*

1. ***The growing need to treat illnesses:*** *New diseases and old diseases resistant to traditional drugs (such as Staph, TB, and Strep) require pharmaceutical companies to spend more money on researching new drugs, over-the-counter drugs, diagnostics and devices, and research and development (spending for research and development increased by 12 percent in 1996 over 1995). The FDA is responding by approving more drugs at a faster rate: In 1996 the agency approved 89 percent more drugs than in the previous year, and did so 10 percent faster. The consumer market is reacting with equal fervor: Pharmaceutical sales in North America grew by 9 percent from 1995 to 1996, generating $82 billion in sales and accounting for one-third of the global industry. In addition, drug companies are lobbying to extend the time they have an exclusive right to sell new products without competition from generic clones. They want this to extend to five years after release—a move that could potentially boost profits by $10 billion.*

given was to be a sponge. Sit there and listen and learn and soak up everything around you. I really saw my first year in the business as a paid internship to learn the industry." Since then she has been promoted several times, worked at two other agencies, and returned to Cline, Davis & Mann as an account supervisor. "I read everything I could about the field, and one of the reasons I got promoted was that I learned the science behind the drugs. I knew all the latest research and became invaluable because I understood things that nobody else did." Most importantly, Wendi discovered

> "Regard your first job as an internship. An education doesn't make you a doctor…for a year or two, you need to learn what the advertising business is all about. The best way to do that is to be hired by an agency so you can follow the 'doctors' around."
>
> *—Lee Clow, chairman, chief creative officer, TBWA/Chiat Day*

that she had a genuine interest in and passion for her work.

"I'm working on products that help people and make a real difference in their lives. That's more rewarding to me than selling toilet bowl cleaner."

Wendi has found that at an entry-level position it's also fairly easy to cross over from a medical to a general agency, and vice versa. The basic jobs and skills are the same. However, she also discovered two important differences in medical advertising that make it more difficult to switch as you gain more experience:

◎ *A lot of medical advertising is not actually advertising, but creating promotional materials and educational materials for patients and physicians. Most account people never work on TV commercials and do not deal with ratings and other media issues. Also, to succeed in medical advertising, it's necessary to understand the scientific and medical aspects of the drug classes you work with as well as a whole slew of FDA issues—which greatly affect legal guidelines for advertising—all of which are much stricter than those governing general advertising. Your knowledge base will become very specific and less applicable to general consumer advertising as time goes on.*

⊚ *There is a shortage of smart, talented account executives in medical advertising, and the good ones tend to be promoted more quickly than in general advertising and earn higher salaries. As a result, switching to a general agency would probably result in a large pay cut as well as a demotion.*

Typically, account executives *do* have a medical background in biology or microbiology, and science education is preferable to marketing. Marketing experience is helpful, but not entirely necessary. Science is an integral part of an account executive's job in a medical agency; it is also very common for an assistant account executive to have several years' experience as a pharmaceutical sales representative. Earning a master's degree in a science-related field can also translate into a higher position.

Most people who start out in pharmaceutical advertising want to be there and have a strong interest in the health sciences. "Don't consider this industry as a back door to getting into a general agency," Wendi warns. "While there once may have been the perception that this field is second tier to general advertising and that people in medical advertising were there because they didn't make it in a consumer shop, this has changed as medical advertising is now a booming business" (see sidebar).

2. **An aging population:** The number of senior citizens is predicted to rise from 37 million to 60 million by 2015. Senior citizens respresent the largest group of phamaceutical users. The managed care industry is aggessively pursuing this market and offering coverage of prescription drugs for the first time. Currently, just 15 percent of Medicare users participate in a managed care plan.

3. **Shift toward managed care:** Analysts predict that managed care organizations will soon exert considerable influence over the pharmaceutical industry. Health Management Offices (HMOs) favor drug treatment as opposed to more costly hospitalization or surgery, and pharmaceuticals represent 9.2 percent of HMOs' health care expenditures, compared to the national average of 7 percent.

# Sales Promotion: Special Offer Experts

## TIM HANLON, SENIOR INTERACTIVE PROJECT MANAGER
### Frankel & Company

U.S. companies spend $70 billion a year on promotion marketing, according to *Promo* magazine. For every dollar spent on advertising, more than two dollars are spent on promotion, making it the single largest portion of the marketing budget. In fact, promotion budgets have surpassed advertising budgets every year since 1974. Promotion is the key element of any marketing plan. Packaged goods providers, service industries, and most other businesses incorporate sales promotion into their marketing plans because it has a measurable impact and is proven to stimulate purchases.

Price, product quality, and brand loyalty are important factors, but they are not the only elements that enter into a consumer's purchase decision. "Consumers want to be wooed," says Chris Sutherland, former director of the Promotions Marketing Association. "Advertising suggests…promotion motivates," he says, and, in fact, studies in supermarkets have shown that three out of four product choices are made after consumers enter the store.

'Buy now! Buy often!' is the motto of the promotion marketer. Sales promotion, designed to motivate an immediate product sale, is the result of combining a consumer product or service with a special offer to motivate a purchase. Promotion involves just about any marketing device—other than advertising—with the main objective to push or pull products through the distribution chain. To be successful, sales promotion must generate measurable "incremental sales," greater than the expected norm. The two major types of sales promotion are price off and value added. A price off promotion is just as it sounds—a temporary price reduction, which actually can take many forms including a sale price ("25 percent off one product" or "buy one get one free"), a coupon delivered through the mail or newspaper via free-standing inserts (FSIs), and a cash rebate, whereby the consumer sends in a proof of purchase to receive a money-back offer.

A value added promotion, on the other hand, offers an extra incentive usually unrelated to the product. Think about how many promotional incentives you've seen, such as sweepstakes: chance drawings from mailed entries; contests: sweepstakes that require some skill, such as writing an essay; and free offers: free items given away with the purchase of a product. Other promotional opportunities include point-of-purchase (POP) displays, promotional products, licensing, sampling, and in-store marketing.

Although the sales promotion business has not been known for its glamour, that notion is changing quickly as interactive technologies become part of the mix. "The digital marketing department at Frankel and Company (one of the country's leading agencies for sales promotion) is probably the most looked at and lusted after division. It's the cool place to be in this business," says Tim Hanlon, the group's senior interactive project manager. "Our company looks at digital marketing as a true barometer of where the future is heading for marketing services as a whole. In the beginning it seemed like only the advertising agencies and media people of the world were affected by interactive technologies, but digital space is exploding with opportunity and affecting virtually every aspect of the marketing mix." Adrienne Skinner, of S&A Associates, a strategic media development company specializing in new media sales, agrees that online promotions is an explosive area. "Promotion marketers cannot hope to find a better avenue than the online world. It is immediate, inexpensive, direct, vast, and interactive. It is also a powerful way to connect to the right people to build relationships," she says.

Frankel started up its digital division in 1996 and is now home to about thirty people. Tim expects that number to double by 1999. "It is unquestionably a great time to break into the business. An entire industry has evolved in the span of four or five years; I don't think any other industry has grown that quickly. Even in an economic downturn, interactive work will continue to go forward and may even keep traditionally cyclical ad agencies afloat. We are just at the beginning of the curve with this technology; it's changing and growing daily."

Tim's department is comprised of four core divisions typical of every interactive shop, making it kind of a mini self-sufficient agency within an agency. The department houses its own independent creative staff; a technology staff schooled in hardware and software issues; an account management staff in charge of understanding classic branding strategies; and a project management staff responsible for micromanaging the day-to-day details and overall process.

> "Advertising is going to be an exciting field for people who love change. You'll have to be an expert at the traditional form—but you'll also have to go beyond what is traditionally known as advertising."
>
> *—Susan Gillette, president, DDB Needham Chicago*

Web programming skills will give you the best edge to break into this business. If you are proficient with some of the more advanced programming languages like JAVA applications, C++, and Perl, you could be seventeen years old and you'll get a phone call, says Tim. If you've got those talents you're going to get a job very easily. In fact, there was a story recently about a Fortune 500 company that found out, to its surprise, that its "web consultant" was a fourteen-year-old boy working out of his bedroom. "There's definitely a compression of experience in this field," Tim observes. "People who have been working two or three years in this business are considered the experts, mainly because it's only a few years old, but then again every expert is only as expert as tomorrow's news because things are constantly changing."

If you don't have any specialized skills, the best entry-level position is on the project management side, advises Tim. "Day to day this means sticking to agendas, making sure people meet deadlines, and general administration. That means attention to detail, following up with the various constituencies, scheduling, communicating needs from various players, interpreting needs from clients or different areas of our department so that everyone's on the same wavelength, and generally facilitating clear communication." This is the best place to be involved in everything going on around you because you are exposed to every aspect of the business. "I can't think of a better path, especially if you have no experience. You will get a little taste of what the client wants, a little taste of the creatives and their frustrations, and a little taste of the account management side and dealing with the client."

Tim took an indirect route into Frankel's interactive department with a peripheral career in media. After graduating in 1988 with a degree in government and English from Georgetown University, he got a job as an assistant media buyer in Leo Burnett's training program. After Burnett he moved around to a couple of other agencies, and then became an associate producer for CBS news. From there Tim returned to USC's Annenberg School for Communication for a master's degree in communications management and then spent two years at an in-house agency for a credit card company. His entry into the interactive field came with his next job at a traditional ad agency; clients were beginning to express interest in interactive technologies, and Tim was able to build the enterprise from the ground up.

> "People who create effective advertising have the ability to come at problems from a fresh perspective. They have a slightly askew point of view and often travel unconventional paths."
>
> *–Tom McElligott, co-founder, Fallon McElligott*

"In the late 1980s there were definitely set tracks for a career in media. Today, the interactive world is less defined and you can easily carve your own path, especially if you have some web experience and skills, whether it's programming or web construction, even if it's your own home page. That is directly applicable."

"I'm probably a little more interested in someone who has a liberal arts education and has gotten the web or marketing or advertising experience outside of the classroom. If you're working at a school paper you're probably grappling with interactive advertising and how to get your paper online. The realities of selling advertising, convincing people of your audience and how you reach them are very fundamental. There's probably no better way to get prepared—in fact you'll probably be better prepared than people who have fifteen or twenty years of experience since they haven't even dealt with the Internet when it comes to advertising and marketing."

Curiosity is a valuable trait in the interactive world and asking questions is an integral part of the work. "The web is so ever-changing that you need to be constantly curious. People who are set in their ways and think they have the whole world figured out are probably not going to be of interest to us."

Tim also likes to see people who are good thinkers, who can think "out of the box," and don't understand the word "no." Advertising, marketing, and promotions are businesses driven by creativity, reflecting a variety of different disciplines, and the web magnifies the need for new ideas. Tim has found that the best meetings come from give-and-take discussions in which people grapple with ideas. To achieve that, "we need people who can think, not just do." But it's more than just having an idea, it's communicating that idea effectively with perspective and maturity, and having the ability to alter it based on new information. These are the elements of critical thinking.

The ideal combination, however, is "classic marketing skills applied to the realities of today's digital marketplace." The older executives know their clients' brands and have the marketing knowledge, but are stumbling along with the interactive component. The young people are coming in cyber-ready and sprouting with new ideas. They understand the latest technologies, but they don't know much about strategic planning, marketing, or demographics. "The magic mix is interactive smarts with classic marketing savvy. The merging of those two core disciplines is the nirvana of this business," emphasizes Tim.

A lot of marketers out there really haven't figured out what the Internet is and what it means to their business, so it's our job to educate them, says Tim. Many are stumbling through this new medium and no one quite has it figured out. "You'd be shocked at some of the traditional blue-chip clients out there who don't get it. They sort of understand, they give it lip service, but they haven't committed the resources and money. Many clients are not sophisticated enough yet to understand how the Internet fits into the overall marketing mix."

As a result, many companies are experiencing what Tim terms an "Internet hangover." A common scenario goes like this—a bright marketing person in the lower levels of the agency begs, borrows, and scrapes money out of various budgets to test out new media. Then, a year later, the big wigs complain that they are not seeing "results," whether that's increased sales or brand awareness. The problem is that the company didn't really think about the project before it went forward—there was no strategic planning behind the Internet initiative. Thus, the results are minimal.

A lot of companies simply adopt a "me-too" strategy, observes Tim. Businesses were simply trying to just draw attention to themselves with a "click here, look at me" mentality,

> "A liberal arts education is an excellent foundation for any advertising person. Because in the course of an advertising career, you will encounter diverse subjects that will serve you well into the future. You need a broad base from which to draw in order to respond effectively. And liberal arts tend to amplify and broaden your awareness."
>
> *–Amil Gargano, co-founder, Ally & Gargano*

and they simply wanted to "count eyeballs." This is changing as companies learn to recognize the utility of the Internet. The airline industry exemplifies this. "Certainly one aspect of the business is brand awareness. There are a lot of news sites and business travel information sites and a wealth of information that some of the key target audiences of an airline would come across, so brand advertising via the web makes a lot of sense. But beyond that there's also great potential for service on airline sites. Ticketing, for example, is a tremendous cost saver. Let's say it takes a ten-minute call on an 800 number to figure out itineraries and pricing. If you can convince someone to buy a ticket on the Internet, you can save the company $30 to $40 dollars. All the intermediary costs of a travel agent or of a customer service agent are gone and you're asking the customer to do most of the work for you. It's the best scenario for a company that is customer intensive. The goal is to convince people to keep coming back to your site to the point where they'll buy a ticket once in a while and then more frequently," says Tim.

Sales promotion can involve hosting a corporate web site, sponsoring a partnering company's site, or co-developing web content with online vehicles designed to deliver entertainment and information. For example, New and Kewl (www.new-kewl.com) showcases innovative products and services along with entertainment programming. Marketers can join in for a fraction of the cost of building an independent site. Parent Soup (www.parentsoup.com), a leading online site for parents, allows advertisers to co-develop editorial content areas, providing them with a unique opportunity to talk with their audience in a way that traditional linear media does not permit.

Because the interactive business is moving so quickly, you have the opportunity to make more money and get promoted much faster than on a typical agency path. At a traditional agency there's definitely a track that begins with grunt work, starting as an account coordinator and handling all the executional work to help the account executives. The interactive field offers a better opportunity to jump in at a higher level, especially if you have experience. It's not uncommon for people to stay with jobs for months instead of years. But with the faster learning curve comes longer hours. A traditional work week at an interactive shop might be 50–70 hours, compared to 40–60 hours at a traditional agency. The Internet is always on. "Don't expect a 9-5, 'let's go golfing at 3:30' job," warns Tim. "People are here because they want to be here, they are intrigued by the space and the potential. It's not quite the Wild West, but there's a lot of uncharted territory to explore."

# *Small Agencies Are Big Business*

## DAN DE GUZMAN, ACCOUNT MANAGER
### The Adstore

Small agencies like the New York-based Adstore are riding the latest trend in advertising, customizing their business to meet the needs of cost-conscious clients by offering ads on a per-project or full-service basis. The concept of operating like a store is new to advertising. Generally, when a client selects an agency of record, the agency creates and produces all of the client's ads and is paid on a monthly retainer; the client is still billed even if no ads are produced during a particular month. But at The Adstore, clients can purchase a TV spot or a print ad with no long-term strings attached.

As international clients seek breakthrough images for their brands, some industry watchers are observing a shift to smaller, more creative ad agencies capable of creating big ideas that can cross borders. Small boutiques are boasting large international accounts: Amster Yard, McCann-Erickson's creative boutique recently won a $15 million assignment to launch a new insurance division for Bancomer, Mexico's largest financial institution. Combined with the $30 million European Bacardi account the agency won in 1996, this fourteen-person shop has brought in $95 million in billings since it opened its doors in 1995. The former Fallon McElligott Berlin won nine of ten new business pitches, including the Bankers Trust, NBA Properties, and Diet Sprite, and pulled in $40 million in billings in 1996.

But others disagree that these assignments represent a trend. "I think too much is being made of this," says Peter Hamilton, executive VP and director of worldwide accounts at McCann-Erickson, the fifth largest agency in the country. "Large advertisers like Unilever want ad agencies that can service their accounts around the world. They don't want just creative boutiques."

Although The Adstore doesn't have the manpower to handle a $20 million international account, technology has leveled the playing ground, allowing this twelve-person shop to act like one of the big agencies and produce advertising consistent in quality with a worldwide agency. This is made possible, in part, by advanced technologies that are extending capabilities once exclusive to large agencies. Small agencies can now efficiently research, store, and transmit large amounts of data. They can generate sophisticated presentation slides, reports, transparencies, animated videos, and graphics—efficiently and cost-effectively. Telecommunications developments also allow small agencies to function like large agencies. Advancements such as remote call forwarding, conference calling, video conferencing, computerized voice mail, e-mail, and digital data transmission are critical to a business that is built on client relationships and interactions, most of which take place by phone. Such devices allow small businesses to look and act much bigger than they really are.

At the same time, bigger is not necessarily better, and the old powerhouses of the ad world like Grey and Y&R are no longer considered to be the movers and shakers. "Today you'd be hard pressed to find a student who aspires to be chair of a Fortune 500 company," observes Amar Bhide, associate professor at Harvard Business School, where half of the students enrolled in an entrepreneurial finance course and one-third of alumni go on to become self employed.[1] The same can probably be said about the aspiring David Ogilvys and Bill Bernbachs: they are not starting out in the mimeograph room and climbing the corporate ladder of behemoth agencies; rather, they are working for a small, interactive multimedia company in somebody's garage.

Outsourcing is another key to the success of small agencies. Although the advertising process follows the same basic flow as in a large agency, the individual procedures are different because certain departments simply do not exist in a small

> " Creativity is not a function of size. Small can be beautiful."
>
> *—David Ogilvy, founder,*
> *Ogilvy & Mather*

[1]Tannenbaulm, Jeffery A., "On Their Own," *The Wall Street Journal*, May 23, 1996, p. R20.

agency. There may be no designated traffic department to keep track of jobs, no research division, and there may not even be a media department. Small agencies often enlist the services of outside market research companies, and media planning and buying is usually outsourced to another company. The Adstore only houses a billing and accounting department, creative division, and account services. Dan *is* the account management department.

Dan began his advertising career in college. After two years of studying physical therapy, Dan transferred to Pace University to earn a bachelor's degree in 1994 in marketing and advertising. At the same time he was working in retail and interned in the marketing department of a clothing company where he learned about media plans and developing marketing proposals. "I decided, why not combine some of my people skills and selling skills and venture into something more creative. I chose advertising."

Dan's first job was with a subsidiary of Grey Advertising, which handles cooperative advertising—a type of advertising in which companies partner to jointly promote their products. He then moved on to Grey Entertainment, working with clients such as Time Warner, but he didn't stay long. "I didn't really care for the politics that are associated with a large agency," he says bluntly, "and I was getting away from the reason I got into advertising in the first place, which was to be where the action is and get my hands dirty. I equate working in a larger agency to being a racehorse in a gate that won't open. You're young and enthusiastic and want to charge ahead, but the bureaucracy holds you back. A small agency exposes you to the entire process—from research to media to creative to client contact. It gives you the opportunity to get your hands into everything and run as far as you want."

But Dan doesn't knock large agencies for the learning experience they provide. "To learn the actual advertising process, a large agency is the best place to be. In a small agency, there's not as much teaching and hand holding. It's wise to learn the basics in a large agency in which the advertising process is a bit more regimented and then bring your knowledge to a small shop."

With just two years under his belt, Dan moved to The Adstore, which resides in a comparatively modest space in the ground floor of a brownstone. The agency handles piecemeal work of large clients such as Coke and Visa, as well as small, local businesses, such as the corner dry cleaning shop. "There is a tremendous amount of variety in working with a small agency," says Dan. "Grey would never handle Maurice's Garment Care business, and as an assistant account executive with a large agency, you could be stuck on a toilet paper account for several years. Many times these small clients are more fun because we have more freedom to take creative risks. We also get to deal with very different types of business people—from the small business entrepreneur to the international conglomerate—and consequently, very different types of consumers."

There are also some less tangible differences between small and large agencies. Small agencies simply have a different feel; some people like it and others don't. "Our atmosphere is communal rather than hierarchical," says Dan. "Smaller agencies don't put any credence in titles because there are no corporate ladders to climb, no corner offices or private bathrooms to aspire to." There are no formal dress codes either in this laid-back office, and even though Dan is the so-called "suit," he is rarely seen wearing one.

In a small agency you also get a lot of opportunities to crosstrain. "At Grey I was exposed to some graphic design programs and learned a bit about production and typesetting; here, I've had the chance to apply that knowledge because our production department isn't really a department, it's just one person. Sometimes I'll get an assignment from a client and actually execute it myself—I would never be able to do that in a larger agency."

Dan is also involved in brainstorming or concepting sessions to give the creatives their strategic direction. He has much more freedom to become involved in the creative process, interact with copywriters and art directors, and share his own ideas—the atmosphere cultivates much more of a team effort. Although the open workspace inspires teamwork and fosters creativity, there is a downside to this small, intimate non-office. "I get along with everyone personally as well as professionally. But if you have any difficulties or tensions with people, you are trapped." There is also less opportunity to hide. You can't help but be seen and you can't get lost in the crowd.

On the plus side, this openness gives you more of an opportunity to shine. "This is part of the beauty of a smaller shop—your performance is easily recognized and rewarded. There is no personnel department to oversee formal reviews, raises, and bonuses. You are in control of your own destiny, and it's up to you to say, 'hey, how am I doing?'" At the same time, it's not quite as easy to gauge your performance without a cushy title to work for, and the opportunity to take on more responsibility is often the sign of advancement rather than specific accolades.

Although Dan doesn't recommend starting out in a small agency right after school, it is possible if you have some knowledge of the advertising process, he says. "Take some advertising and marketing classes in school so you understand the basic terms we use in the business and how an agency operates." There are opportunities for assistant account executives and account coordinators, as well as administrative assistants on the account management side, says Dan. If you take an entry-level position at a small firm, salaries are comparable to what you would earn in a large agency. A typical entry-level account person writes status reports, helps to develop creative briefs, and assists with media planning. There is a fair amount of grunt work and not much glamour, but everything in a small agency has a purpose and it's part of a larger picture. You will never feel like you're pushing papers or killing time, says Dan. It's tougher to break into the creative side because small boutiques are known for their ads that push the limits, and everyone wants to work in a place that worships creative freedom.

Small shops also employ freelancers, particularly when the work load gets heavy. The Adstore will often add up to three freelancers, essentially expanding its staff by 20 percent. "We treat freelancers like part of our staff—when we bring someone in, they work side by side with us rather than under us," says Rob.

Computer skills are necessary to get in the door, and many smaller agencies use MacIntosh computers. It's essential to know Microsoft Word, Excel, and Quark, says Dan. Be willing to do anything to learn, be open to new ideas, and above all, be an exciting, charismatic, upbeat, fun person—personality is very important in the tight-knit, intimate atmosphere of a small agency because everyone works together so closely. "We don't want any prima donnas," warns Dan. "Expect your first year to be a low-paid learning experience, so be a sponge and absorb everything around you. If you're looking to make a lot of money right out of school, this is not the place for you. You've really got to love advertising...if you love learning about what it takes to press people's buttons, then you're in the right business."

An internship will definitely give you a competitive advantage, particularly if you've worked in a large agency. Real world experience counts for a lot, says Dan. "If you intern in a smaller shop, you'll end up with the grunt work, spend your time gophering, and won't learn much. Larger agencies have established programs for interns, often rotating students through different departments and exposing them to different jobs."

Nearly all small agencies, even one- or two- person shops are listed in the *Standard Directory of Advertising Agencies*. Dan recommends writing directly to the agency's president or general manager with job inquiries that are specifically targeted to each agency, illustrating your interest in and knowledge of the particular business. "Or better yet, walk in the door. Show up in person, drop off your resume, and give us your best sales pitch."

# Direct Marketing: Narrowing the Target

## MICHAEL GOLDSTEIN, ACCOUNT SUPERVISOR
*Draft*Worldwide

Direct marketing was first practiced by Benjamin Franklin in 1744 when he mailed a small catalog offering some 600 books. It has come a long way since then; today, direct marketing generates $1.2 trillion in total sales, according to The WEFA Group, a leading economic forecasting organization. Total direct marketing sales in the U.S. grew at an annual rate of 8.1 percent between 1992 and 1997, and five years from now, sales are projected to hit more than $1.8 trillion, with industry growth outpacing sales in the overall U.S. economy. About $153 billion will be spent this year on direct response advertising, which is more than half of all advertising dollars spent in America, and more than 20 million U.S. jobs are related to direct response sales and advertising activity.[1]

Direct marketing is broadly defined as "any direct communication to a customer or business designed to generate a direct order, a lead, or traffic."[2] It employs and integrates all forms of media, including telemarketing, mail, television, radio, newspapers, magazines, and the Internet. Direct marketing is essen-

---

[1]Wientzen, Bob, President and CEO, Direct Marketing Association, excerpted from speech at The DMA Investment Community Conference, Chicago, IL, October 6, 1997.

[2]Ibid.

## Direct Marketing and the Internet

*Manufacturers dominated the marketplace in the 1950s and 1960s and retailers took over in the 1970s and 1980s. Today it's customers who are driving business into the next century as technology becomes a pervasive force. The "we make it, you take it" sales motto of previous decades has now been replaced by a marketing mentality in which businesses integrate consumer preferences and feedback to continuously modify and improve products and services.*

*This customer-driven market is fueled by the Internet, and as an analyst at Forrester Research Inc., a Massachusetts-based computer consulting and research firm, asserts, "If you're not using the Internet today, you probably won't be in business in the 21st century." The Internet is certainly the hottest new addition to the direct marketing mix and affords cost-effective business-to-business as well as business-to-consumer communication for a wide range of markets. It is the most global, yet personal, way to reach customers. A recent Direct Marketing Association study found that 81 percent of more than 400 direct marketing professionals anticipate increasing investment in electronic commerce within three years.*

*Expenditures for online marketing stood at $275 million in 1997 and are expected to grow by a whopping 66 percent annually to reach $3.5 billion by the year 2002. Interactive sales, which stood at $1.9 billion in 1997, are predicted to increase by 75 percent per year. As a result, employment in this field is estimated to jump by 66 percent each year over the next five years.*

tially a business tool—a testable, measurable, and accountable means of selling goods and services.

Because 80 percent of business is generated by 20 percent of customers, all marketing-related disciplines are going to become "directed" as businesses move toward building relationships in addition to building brands, says Laurie Spar, vice president of the Direct Marketing Educational Foundation. As a result, some are now defining direct marketing as "a comprehensive system of media and methods designed to elicit a response from a prospect or customer in order to develop or enhance a 'client relationship.'"

Direct marketing gains nothing by selling one product to one person at a time. The goal of direct marketing is to create a database of customers to whom you can sell additional products at higher response rates and with greater cost effectiveness. This process begins by converting a "prospect" into a "customer" with an initial sale. Once the customer becomes a "client," customer service and follow-up are used to turn the client into an "advocate"—a source of new sales to other prospects through word of mouth.[3]

The key to direct marketing is the offer, not the product, and it encompasses much more than just price. The offer consists of everything that impacts the value or perceived value of the product or service and everything that impacts the process of getting it from the seller to the buyer. It's the "deal" or the "hook"—the free trial, demo, special issue, video, calculator, sweepstakes prize or ginsu knives.

Advertising and direct marketing only have one thing in common: the English language. Here's why:

- ◎ *Advertising builds awareness and is a conduit for a sale at some other time and place. Direct marketing makes an immediate sale or contact directly with the customer, at a time and place controlled by the seller.*

- ◎ *Advertising is only mildly measurable; direct marketing is totally accountable. Every response is measured including cost per order, cost per lead, and the dollar value of a customer.*

- ◎ *Advertising sells products; direct marketing sells offers.*

- ◎ *Advertising creates markets, direct marketing discovers them.*

[3]Duncan, George, "Direct Mail and the Dynamics of Response, Part I: The Interactive Medium," Direct Marketing News Online.

- *Advertising tries to influence behavior, direct marketing seeks to repeat it.*

- *Advertising is an art; direct marketing is a science, with the goal of documenting all the variables, testing the results, and replicating them.*[4]

> **" I worked on all those horrible projects nobody wanted. I did ads for crutch tips—those little rubber tips on the bottom of crutches—and ostomy bags. You don't get the glamorous assignments when you start."**
>
> *–Don Easdon, founder, Heaten/Easdon*

Many years ago David Ogilvy, founder of Ogilvy & Mather, advised advertising agencies not to hire anyone unless they had direct response experience. "Direct marketers know what works," he said. Michael Goldstein took this advice and turned it into a career. He decided to pursue advertising after a college internship at Grey and with a degree in speech communications from Syracuse University, he started as a secretary at McCaffrey and McCall in 1991, now part of Bates USA. "It was a humbling experience to burst out of school full of motivation only to fax and file and type for $17,000. And while it was humiliating, I feel like I did need that experience. I learned to be self-confident rather than arrogant, and there is a big difference."

Michael believes there are more opportunities today to break into the business above the secretarial level, and he sees young people starting in traffic or as an assistant account executive. "It's based on need as well as the mindset that if young people come in with sharp skills, we want to utilize them appropriately."

After six months at McCaffrey, Michael found that he liked the bottom-line, results-oriented nature of the business and moved to Wunderman, where he climbed the ranks from account coordinator to assistant account executive to account executive before coming to *Draft*Worldwide.

A direct agency is staffed much the same way as a traditional ad agency with an account management, creative, media, research, and traffic department. In addition, many agencies have a database and interactive division. As an account supervisor for a direct marketing agency, Michael's job responsibilities differ very little from the same position at a traditional agency. *Draft*Worldwide also has a department called Data Technologies Services whose primary function is to build customer databases. Process management, modeling, operations, telemarketing, and fulfillment are part of this group's responsibility.

*For direct marketers, whose livelihoods depend on in-depth market knowledge, the Internet is particularly useful for:*

- *gathering information about customer demographics and buying preferences, making databases more timely and relevant*

- *targeting new goods and services to customers*

- *reaching new markets*

- *expediting the purchase process, delivery, customer service, and feedback from customers*

- *managing back-office functions more efficiently, e.g., providing company-wide access to real-time data and facilitating transmission of information.*[1]

[1]"1997 Economic Impact: U.S. Direct Marketing Today, Executive Summary," The Direct Marketing Association Online.

[4]Ibid.

Breaking into direct marketing may be easier because there is less competition and more opportunity to start at a higher level. At the same time, it is also more difficult because the business requires some specific skills. "You need to have analytical abilities in addition to strategic skills, and a strong orientation towards numbers is critical to support that," says Michael.

The ability to understand consumer behavior is another essential skill. "There is a shift from talking to customers to listening to customers and partnering with consumers rather than targeting them," observes Laurie Spar. "You can absolutely leverage any retail experience you've had that entails day-to-day, face-to-face interaction with customers." Working one on one with consumers, even if you're behind a counter or a cash register, is the first step in understanding and analyzing their needs, a key factor in direct response advertising.

Although you think you may not have learned much from your summer jobs, they do demonstrate responsibility. Throughout high school Michael had a variety of jobs, from delivering food to washing cars. "If that's all you've got, put it on your resume," he says. "I don't expect someone to have incredible job experience coming right out of college, but I like to see someone who is out there working, who gets involved in things, who tries to learn something, and isn't afraid to get their hands dirty."

> "I hire people I like. That may sound stupid, but personality counts."
>
> *—Stan Richards, founder,*
> *The Richards Group*

Michael also likes to see someone who brings good thoughts to the table and isn't afraid to make mistakes. Communication skills are another important element. "How you communicate with me reflects how you will communicate with a client." But all skills aside, personality is just as important, says Michael. "The skills are significant, but you can teach skills to someone at the entry level. I like to see someone who is outgoing and excited about the business—an interesting and charismatic person who I'm going to get along with. If you're not a fun person, you're not going to make it through the rest of my interview. Fun is a top skill for entry level." Most people don't realize that their boss is going to spend as much if not more time with them than with their own family and friends. "So if you want me to teach you the business, I want to have fun doing it."

Starting out as an assistant account executive is a good way to learn the direct marketing process, from reviewing mechanicals to being involved in the creative development. Assistant account executives are responsible for billing, maintaining the client's budget, and handling invoices. Their main job is to ensure that the account is operational. "You are doing everything, just at lower levels by beginning as a silent partner. As you learn more, you will have the chance to speak up." Traffic is another avenue for people who want to move into account services, says Michael, and it's a natural grooming ground because you get a bird's eye view of the entire process.

To begin in the creative department you certainly need to demonstrate your original thinking with a strong portfolio, but there is more that goes into the mix than sheer creativity. Creatives are salespeople, and the catalog, direct mail piece, or web site is the showroom. Copywriters need to be skilled at selling a benefit rather than an image, and they need to master the art of "the offer" with an in-depth knowledge of a product and its target audience.

Laurie finds that students don't realize that their job searches are really a form of direct marketing. "This is your first attempt to sell a product—yourself—through a direct mail campaign. The idea of building a database of employers, testing your concept, and selling yourself with benefits is the same process you will use on the job."

# *Interactive Advertising: Click on a Career*

## ROB GOERGEN, ACCOUNT DIRECTOR
### Thunder House Online Marketing Communications

Computers and Internet access are now available in our businesses and schools, airplanes and cafes...even our underwear! That's right, for just $3,000 you too can sew computer components into your underwear like Steven Mann of MIT, and imbed the monitor into your glasses, a system he recently showcased at the First International Symposium on Wearable Computers.

Nobody is certain exactly how many people are on the Internet—a recent Roper poll found that 20 million Americans are wired, while a study by Find/SVP believes the number to be as high as 31 million. Nor are we sure how much time people spend online. But we do know one thing: The Internet empowers individuals by providing instant access to information and a capacity for direct dialogue, and it is a breakthrough technology that will continue to evolve and change every aspect of our lives. A whole new realm of possibilities is on the horizon for advertisers as they explore the options of communicating with customers electronically, and interactive advertising is one of the most exciting and challenging new opportunities in the industry.

Nearly every major agency has an interactive arm or is in the process of developing a presence in the field. Some, like Saatchi & Saatchi and Young & Rubicam, have in-house staff who report to the media director. Others, such as Bozell, are establishing sister agencies; Poppe Tyson handles interactive

## What's New on the Net?

*"Cybersoaps" are the latest form of entertainment on the Web and a smart new opportunity for advertisers who want to capture a repeat audience. While some companies simply place banner ads, others, like Rubin Postaer and its client, American Honda, are actually writing themselves and their products into the storyline script. Advertisers have tremendous freedom in this arena; there are essentially no standards regulating advertising on the Internet, as opposed to television, which is governed by the FCC.*

*A new cybersoap — an online daily soap opera — about the trials and tribulations of a Madison Avenue ad agency, affords advertisers even more creative license. Whitehall-Robins Healthcare, a unit of American Home Products Corp., is sponsoring "475 Madison Avenue" on the Microsoft Network for one year and will use the venue to advertise Advil, Dimetapp, Robitussin, and Centrum products.*

*This innovative marketing technique is as new as...the 1930s, when the soap opera first earned its name. The first radio soap opera, **Oxydol's Own Ma Perkins**, was produced by Proctor and Gamble and named for its soap sponsor, Oxydol. Proctor and Gamble went on to produce **Guiding Light**, **As the World Turns**, and **Another World**.[1]*

[1]Lever, Jane, "Advertising: With Soap Operas on the Web, What's Next?" *AdAge Online*, March 11, 1996.

work for Bozell's clients and pursues its own new business. Other groups, such as Omnicom, are buying percentages of big agencies like Red Sky Interactive and Razorfish. In addition to the big powerhouses, lots of small, hot shops are popping up everywhere you look, and they are successfully stealing away the big guys' blue-chip clients. Some industry analysts believe these houses can succeed by staying small, keeping their costs low, and turning out a sharp, creative product. Others think they will have to ally themselves with large agencies, consolidate, or disappear. Don't tell this to Modem Media of Westport, Connecticut, which handles interactive work for MasterCard International and AT&T, among others—earning revenues in the low tens of millions.

What does interactive advertising entail? The term was originally used to describe advertising that called for one-to-one communication between marketer and consumer or manufacturer and consumer. It did not mean technology-based marketing, but it just so happened that the use of advanced technology was the most efficient way to do so. But only several years ago, many of the first generation web sites merely offered promotional information by repositioning annual reports or press releases, or simply transplanting their print ads.

Web banner ads used to sit quietly on the screen, begging Web surfers to "click me." Today they are more dimensional, inviting viewers to play games; sign up for product samples, place orders and buy products using pull-down menus; search databases; and enter sweepstakes. Companies like AT&T have even developed "talkies" that use both sound and video in their ads. What does the future hold? The next step is mini-commercials, known in the trade as "interstitial" advertisements, which are already appearing on sites such as MSNBC and *Hotwired Magazine*.[1] Can ads based on a television model successfully be replicated in an interactive medium? And will users, accustomed to total freedom, tolerate the intrusion? That remains to be seen, as interactive advertisers, including Rob Goergen, grapple with these dynamic issues.

"This is a business for independent thinkers," says Rob. "We want people who can generate and execute original ideas. But you should also be productive in a team environment because you'll be surrounded by people with very different backgrounds, interests, and goals, and we all have to work together. It's not just the agency working with the client; it's much more of a group effort—I.T. [information technology] professionals, sales professionals, the operations people, the fulfillment people."

[1]  McDonnell, Sharon, "Web Ads Add Interactivity to Lure Surfers," *Adage Online*, Sept. 13, 1997.

Yet an interactive agency is structured much like a typical consumer agency. "At McCann Interactive, we operate very similarly to a traditional agency with account execs, creatives, maybe even a media planner or a buyer, and they all work together to complete a project. The difference is that we have an in-house producer who is the team leader in terms of project management and the production process, as an account executive might be. The department is very large in terms of an interactive agency: there are 15 people in our New York office, 40 in the Cambridge office, and probably about 200 people worldwide," says Rob.

Rob began his career in 1994 in the business development division of McCann-Erickson, "a time when the web was just starting to become an influential piece of the marketing mix but wasn't really showing any mature signs yet of becoming a marketing vehicle," Rob recalls. When a senior executive asked him to join the new interactive division, he jumped at the chance to become part of McCann-Erickson's new digital communications venture. Starting as an assistant account executive, Rob quickly rose from account executive to account director in just three years. "This would not happen at a general agency, but everything was moving so quickly. I probably fit into a pretty rare group, not necessarily because I happened to be any better than anyone else, but because I happened to be in the right place at the right time and took advantage of a unique opportunity."

> **"I like to see people try the unexpected."**
>
> *—Mike Koelker, corporate director of creative development, Foote, Cone & Belding*

In fact, Rob had no background in technology. He did have "net" experience...in tennis, that is. After graduating from the University of Richmond in 1993 with a major in history and a concentration in Spanish, he joined the pro tennis tour for a year and a half. He did a lot of reading while traveling and discovered an interest in marketing and advertising, which built on his sales and retail experience during college.

"Marketing experience is much more valuable than technical experience in this field," asserts Rob. "I look for someone who has a marketing background—maybe you've studied it in school, maybe you've had another job in a traditional ad agency, maybe you've worked on the client side. I look for individuals who are capable of broadening their expertise, expanding their horizons. You should be open-minded enough to learn about technology because account executives need to be adept at discussing technological issues and able to give viewpoints to their clients. It's a bit like television—an advertising executive recommends how to use the medium, but he doesn't have to explain how the TV works, or how the cathode ray tubes function inside the television. With interactive advertising, we have to talk conceptually about load times and browsers although we don't have to have technical expertise."

Marketing skills are based on solid communication skills, which can be honed by working in any type of business or internship. "Communication skills are composed of five main elements," says Rob. "I look at someone's oral and written skills, their interpersonal skills, their ability to make clear and concise statements, their capacity to have a point of view, and their general poise. The best way to demonstrate these skills is to be able to explain a project that you managed from beginning to end. Anecdotes are very meaningful—demonstrate how you developed a concept, how the concept was matured, how it was executed, and what your viewpoint was on the results of the project."

Solid computer skills are also essential for an entry-level position. Spreadsheets, Powerpoint, and Microsoft Word are necessary and a familiarity with the web and its language is also important. "We practice what we preach—we do all our presentations and reviews online, and electronic mail has replaced regular mail. All of our work is networked-based with shared resources and shared projects. We will use copywriters from our Cambridge, Massssachusetts, office and artists from New York, and we'll meet once in person during the life of a project. It's extraordinarily effective to use the web for business purposes, and it cuts back on a tremendous amount of xeroxing, mailing, filing, phone calling. It is essential for an entry-level employee to seamlessly manage electronic communication and 'virtual' administration."

Secretaries, receptionists, and group assistants are the classic entry-level, promotable positions; assistant account executives typically have six months or a year of advertising experience under their belt. In addition to junior copywriters and art directors, McCann hires junior producers to organize production timelines, manage budgets, orchestrate the creative team, and run the studio.

Assistant account executives are responsible for a variety of research tasks, from tracking web site success and audience measurement to analyzing the competition. "Clients are always asking, 'What's going on in the market? What is the competition doing? What is happening in terms of new technology?' We have to keep clients abreast of these issues," says Rob. "In addition to traditional assistant account executive duties, such as budget and invoice management, we give our junior-level account people a lot of responsibility for dealing with clients, writing points of view, or maybe working with senior staffers to develop a perspective on a new technology development, such as Java or Shockwave."

Junior employees will hone their ability to collect, analyze, and synthesize information to solve problems creatively. "You need to know how to go beyond the initial source to retrieve research; if you hit a dead end, you need to know where you can turn. The web is a phenomenal source for research information that is applicable to our industry."

During your first year it's also critical to learn how to act within an agency-client environment. Working with clients involves understanding the medium, the environment, and the competitive landscape, in addition to the client's product and strategic goals, to provide sound business decisions. But there are also less tangible skills that one needs to know in dealing with clients, such as learning how and when to give an honest and sensitive point of view. Rob has learned that "advertising is a service business and a lot of things have to do with etiquette, knowing how to give your opinion and when to steer the client back on track."

Time management is another important skill. "We are a small agency and even at McCann you don't have a boss or supervisor or director overseeing you 24 hours a day. You've got to learn how to handle your own projects and how to manage your own time and resources. You also have to be sensitive to working as part of a team environment. That's something we really stress to our junior-level people."

> "People who think advertising is about writing good ads will be disappointed. Advertising is about solving problems for clients."
>
> —*Susan Gillette, president, DDB Needham Chicago*

A lot of these skills are transferable to traditional consumer shops, but Rob believes that it's easier to make the move from a general agency to an interactive one rather than vice versa. "In these lean and mean interactive agencies, you learn a lot of skills but you're not learning them as well or as in depth as you would at a general agency. If you're going from an interactive to a general agency, you may have to take a step back before you can take a step forward."

Starting out at a general shop is also a good way break into its interactive division; because these small departments usually don't have their own personnel resources, requests for employees are sent to the general agency's human resources staff.

Once you have your foot in the door, it's much easier to make a lateral move. McCann Interactive also posts notices for new positions in newsgroups and on the web where people might be searching for a job, such as the New York New Media Association.

This is a very exciting time to break into interactive advertising, and it's much easier to do so now than it was just several years ago. "No one was putting any money into the web in 1994 and even early 1995 when I started out," Rob recalls. $480 million was spent on web advertising in 1997, and though this is just a tiny fraction of the $170 billion advertisers spent in traditional media, this number is up sharply from $150 million in 1996 and growing very quickly. Projections estimate ad spending on the Web to reach $5 billion by the year 2000.[2]

Interactive advertising speaks to a new breed of consumer, one who is significantly more educated about a product or service prior to the purchase. Rob notes, "People are enlightened and empowered before they walk into that automotive dealer, for example. They're armed with as much information as the automotive dealer himself might know in terms of what their options are, what the blue book values are, what accessories they can get. In some cases they're not going to go to the dealer at all. They're just going to use something like Dealernet or Auto-by-Tel. How do we communicate with these highly sophisticated consumers and how do we hold their attention? These issues are at the forefront of interactive advertising because it is not a "hard sell" atmosphere; we have consumers who may spend 10–20 minutes with us on a web site as opposed to the 30 seconds it takes to read a magazine ad."

> " You can't achieve any kind of greatness in the ad business unless you change the business, or add something to the business, or reinvent the business, or simply break the rules of the business. Because that's what creativity is."
>
> *–Tom Monahan, formerly of Leonard Monahan Lubards & Kelly*

Interactive advertising affords the rare opportunity to develop new practices, new programs, new systems, and new techniques, says Rob. "Granted, they're all grounded in marketing 101's basic strategic thinking, but there are a lot of new developments out there. I'm not using the same methodologies or practices that people have used for the past hundred years. Working in an environment where you are a pioneer is the chance of a lifetime."

[2]Richtel, Matt, "TV-Type Ads Emerge on the Web," *AdAge Online*, Apr. 19, 1997.

# *Automotive Agencies: Driving the Deal*

## STAN SMITH, MARKETING ANALYST/AUTOMOTIVE
### W.B. Doner

Cars are kind of like watches: they come in different shapes and sizes, styles and colors. Some are automatic, others manual, and although they all are designed to tell the time, a Rolex is very different from a Timex. Likewise, a car is much more than its hardware. A car is not a product. It is a solution to a problem, namely getting you from point A to point B safely, comfortably, and efficiently.

Although automotive technology and design has not changed significantly over the past fifty years, consumers certainly have, according to Stan Smith, marketing analyst for W.B. Doner, Ford Motor Company's leading ad agency. With the help of technology, consumers are becoming more knowledgeable about their purchases, and they are using the Internet to get a leg up on dealers. Consumers are armed with information—in some cases they even know what the dealer paid for the vehicle—and it puts them in a much more savvy position to negotiate a car deal, explains Stan.

Online services like Auto-by-Tel and Dealernet are also revolutionizing the process of purchasing a car. These car-search services allow consumers to plug in information online and find a particular vehicle. You can even purchase your car online through Auto-by-Tel. The only time consumers actually need to have interaction with the dealership is when they go in to pick up the car. People who are uncomfortable with the dealership experience can manage the entire purchase process from the comfort of their own home.

Stan notes, "We are seeing that 20 percent of buyers actually purchase their cars through these types of services, and the automotive industry is changing to meet these growing demands. Chrysler is testing various ways that people can purchase their vehicles online, and dealers are setting up web sites to become part of the information exchange. In the future, people may go right to a dealership web site for the information they need and buy their car from the individual dealer who would still make money from the exchange." New services such as these are what many in automotive advertising now spend their time researching, creating, and promoting, as demand for these services is on the rise.

More than ever, it is critical to understand consumers and their multifaceted approach to purchasing a car. "We exhaustively research the consumer and our work engages social and cultural levels as well as the economics of the car purchase," says Stan. He also sees the Internet as a valuable tool to gauge how consumers are approaching their experiences. Chat rooms are an invaluable resource to be able to peek in and see what people are saying about their experiences. Stan will look at how often consumers visit a certain web site to get an idea of what kind of information they're seeking out in their research. Online classified ads also yield a wealth of information—to learn even more about the consumer, market analysts can simply call people and ask them why they are selling their car.

Cars have a long purchase cycle, and the goal is to create a dialogue with the consumer and build a relationship rather than just close a sale. "We know that when a person first starts to look at a car, they start to build their information about six weeks before the actual purchase. They begin researching, visiting dealers, they ask Mom and Dad. Our goal, especially for people who do their research online, is to initiate that relationship with them at the beginning of that phase and then use the Internet as a tool throughout that entire process to tailor our communications to them. Consumers are saying that they want this long-term interaction. They want to know that the manufacturer is with them from cradle to grave," Stan believes.

Until recently, the automotive business focused simply on hardware with a straightforward advertising model: Show the car and communicate its product features and benefits. But a new paradigm is emerging with interactive marketing that shifts the emphasis to the "software" components of the business, such as the experience of buying a car. Saturn is a perfect example of a company using this principle by playing on the experience of purchasing and owning a car; Infiniti doesn't even show the car in some of their commercials.

All cars are essentially alike—it's the brand and personality of a car that distinguishes one from the next. Is your car a status symbol or a symbol of freedom? Do you slide into rich leather seats and drive while listening to an aria, or do you roll down your windows and kick up some dirt? "The difference between a Ford Taurus and a Pop-Tart is that you have a real emotional connection to your product, and a larger range of emotions are built into the purchase. Brand management is the paradigm we work with to connect the brand with the consumer. We give a lot of attention to what exactly the brand is saying, it's personality, and how it relates to our target buyer."

The agency's job is to convince you to buy into a car emotionally, and this is more important than ever with the advent of outlets such as Car Max, Autonation, and Driversmart. These retailers do not group vehicles according to nameplate or brand. Rather, they place all different makes of cars side by side so that all the trucks are together and all sports cars are together. This setup is the same as Circuit City (which owns Car Max): all the large-screen televisions are together; all the VCRs are together. As a result, cars now have to fight for "shelf space" just like detergents, and branding is more important than ever.[2]

With such vast changes taking place in the automotive industry, there is tremendous opportunity for young people to contribute to the business. Before joining Doner as a marketing analyst, Stan spent just two years honing his interactive marketing skills after graduating in 1995 with a degree in political science from Miami University in Oxford, Ohio. He was hired into Doner's marketing department, which handles much of the account planning for the Ford Dealer associations, and because of his previous Internet experience, his job began to shift toward the interactive end of the business.

"I sold myself as a person who had experience in an interactive field to an agency that was starting to grow its interactive capabilities. This is a skill that's invaluable right now, and I know for sure that it set me apart. At the same time, I think there's merit to being a well-rounded person and having a variety of different experiences and viewpoints." Stan's resume had a subsection he called "Areas of Effectiveness." "Even though I only had two years of experience working in this field, I identified some areas in which I thought I could be effective and contribute to the agency. You are your very first product

[2]Patty, Tom, President, World Wide Nissan Account Director, TBWA/ Chiat Day Online.

and your resume is your very first type of advertising. This is your first opportunity to sell yourself before you go ahead and sell someone else's product, and you have to position yourself to be able to fill a niche in the advertising market. You have to set yourself apart from others by taking a serious look at who you are and how you can contribute to the team you want to join."

We like to see people who can handle a lot of different projects in different arenas at the same time, says Stan, and this is a practical skill that you can hone in college. "Particular to the auto industry, I look for a person who shows the ability to learn quickly and take initiative. You have to take it upon yourself to get the information that you need to be effective in your job. I also look for a person who really has a passion for advertising. You may bounce around a bit before settling into an automotive account, and you need to have a passion to deal with all of the areas that you may be placed in. This is a very fast-paced, high-energy environment and a person who has a passion for advertising will stay for the long term."

In the auto industry it is essential to understand the client's product, exactly what they're selling, who they're selling to, and get a good feel for what consumers want. This is a lot for a young person to grasp before they can really be effective on an automotive account, observes Stan. The typical entry-level candidate begins as a traffic coordinator. This position provides a good knowledge base because it exposes you to every department and every element of the advertising process. It is also possible to start out as an assistant media planner or an assistant account executive, which is one rung up from a traffic coordinator.

An automotive account offers a lot of exciting challenges. "The industry is evolving quickly and as a result, we are dealing with new and complex issues. In Michigan, the automotive industry is the focal point of our lives, but there is never a dull moment." Even though Stan focuses on the interactive end of the business, he is very involved in the account's overall focus

> " It is important to have time away from your agency, time to travel, read, go to films, listen to music…all those experiences will make you a better ad person. It gives you material to draw on. Dull people make dull ads."
>
> *—Nancy Rice, senior vice president, group creative director, DDB Needham, Chicago*

> " The most important thing about the whole ad game is to make damn sure you're really passionate about it. It's no place for people who aren't sure they want to be here."
>
> *—Tom McElligott, co-founder Fallon McElligott*

and development. Market researchers are no longer buried beneath piles of data, and he supports the account teams daily by providing them with a point of view. You are on the front line in terms of presenting your work and being involved in the decision-making process, says Stan. You are much more up front in terms of strategic planning and management.

Technology is growing by leaps and bounds and savvy market researchers who understand new media developments are in demand. "They say what takes a year to develop in real time takes three months in Internet time. Right now, for example, you can take a virtual walk around a car on Toyota's Web site, get in the car and see the dashboard. This technology is in its infancy right now, but I believe that we'll see some very advanced and compelling developments in the near future."

# *Corporate Advertising: The In-House Track*

## VICKY VITARELLI, ADVERTISING MANAGER
### MasterCard

Why do you use MasterCard instead of Visa? Prefer Coke to Pepsi? Wear Calvins rather than Levi's? Is an Oreo more than just a cookie to you?

What is the difference between a product and a brand? A product is tangible—you can see it and touch it. It has physical attributes such as features and price. A brand is the part of the product you can't put in a box. According to Ogilvy & Mather, known for such renowned brands as American Express and Hershey, "A brand is how consumers feel about a product; the affection they feel for it, the personality they ascribe to it, the trust and loyalty they give it. Above all—the shared experience they have with it."

A brand has an identity and a personality. Some are down to earth and friendly, like Hallmark and Kodak; others are rugged and spirited, like Nike and Marlboro. Brands also satisfy needs—an American Express card makes you feel privileged; Calvins make you sexy. Brands are alive and dynamic, yet intangible, and therefore extremely valuable.

The true goal of advertising is to create a brand by initiating communication that leads to the development of a lifelong relationship between the product and the consumer. "We are paid to enhance the relationship between a product and its users...to place that product meaningfully, respectfully in people's lives...through all our communications efforts. That is

## Branding

*Industries undergoing dramatic change, such as telecommunications and technology, have the greatest need and opportunity to build brand strategies. With such a vast array of choices for consumers, it is critical for companies to build brand identity and loyalty. Brands are even more important in technology markets than in retail because those purchasing decisions have greater ramifications — technology choices intimately affect the way companies run their business from the bottom up.*

*"For many years, technology marketers could build a better mousetrap, then sit back and watch the customers line up at their door. Those days are gone," says Chuck Pettis, senior vice president of EvansGroup Technology, the ad agency's specialty division. Slapping "new and improved" on a product will no longer inspire customers to line up at your door. Consumers need to feel confident and secure about their purchases and the role that technology plays in their lives.*

*Branding is even more important in mature technology markets where cost advantages are increasingly harder to develop. How can your product compete when all of the major players in your industry have made similar cuts in their corporate costs? Brand equity is what makes the difference — the added value provided to a product or company by its brand name. It is the financial advantage of a brand over a generic or less worthy brand. Software is more valuable if it is from Microsoft or Lotus, for example. A computer is more valuable if it has an Intel chip inside.*

*How important is branding to Microsoft's mission? "We believe we've achieved the mind share of the customers as seeing Microsoft as the leading company, not only in the software industry, but in the personal computing industry. We want to build on that leadership with a reputation for innovative products that make people's lives better, improve their overall productivity, and are fun to use," says Marty Taucher, former director of public relations for Microsoft.*

how a product earns a right to become a brand," according to Charlotte Beers, chairman emeritus of Ogilvy & Mather.

Brands uniquely identify a company and its products, differentiating them from competitors, and Vicky Vitarelli's job is to convince consumers to make purchases with MasterCard rather than Visa, American Express, checks, or cash. "People are bombarded with hundreds of messages every day and they are more sophisticated than ever about the choices they make and the products they use. My job is to tell people how our product will make a difference in their lives."

Vicky began her advertising career in 1992 in the media buying department of Ogilvy & Mather, where she purchased local TV spots for the ad agency. "At first I didn't know that I wanted to work in advertising, and I certainly didn't understand the structure of an agency. But I knew that I wanted to learn more about the agency and the advertising process as a whole."

Vicky switched departments and moved into media planning in an effort to do more strategic than execution-type work. After a year and a half and with a continued desire to understand the "bigger picture," she moved into account management at another agency, Bozell, where she worked her way up to account executive. While working on the Bausch & Lomb account, the client asked the agency if they could "borrow" her for several months to assist with their marketing plan. "This happens every once in a while in the business," says Vicky, "and it's a great opportunity to gain experience on the client side. Advertising is just one component of the marketing process. I wanted to be closer to where the decisions are made and part of the entire marketing plan, so I jumped at the chance."

After getting a taste of life on the client side of advertising, Vicky took her agency experience to MasterCard's corporate ad department. A corporate advertising department works with the company's advertising agency to develop a strategy and to create advertising based on the company's mission to achieve its goals—from increasing sales, to creating a new product, to developing a new market for an old product.

Vicky is driven by the process of understanding the ways in which people make decisions. "I love watching people in stores and am fascinated by the way they choose their products. I was recently standing in line to pay for something and the woman in front of me asked, 'Do you accept checks?' My first thought was, 'Why isn't she using a credit card and what do I need to do to get her to change her mind!?' To love the advertising business, you've got to love studying what makes people tick and have an exhaustive urge to dissect human behavior."

Corporate advertising is the place to be if you are a leader, problem solver, and strategic thinker. Your job is to educate people about your product and influence their purchase decisions, and you should enjoy the challenge of competing with rival businesses to have an impact on consumers' decisions. Like executives on the agency side, Vicky also speaks of having a passion for her work and the products she promotes. "Could I spend my day developing strategies to sell something I don't believe in? Probably not. To really embrace your work, you must have a passion for your product that will extend to the consumer." In other words, if you think that advertising is a manipulative process that convinces people to buy things they don't really need so that companies can make money, you should think twice about working in this field. If, however, you believe that advertising is a cost-effective means to reach consumers and educate them about products that can improve their lives, then you are in the right business.

There are two schools of thought on breaking into the client side of advertising. On one hand, you need to have a solid understanding of advertising and the process to manage and direct your company's advertising agency. The best way to do this is to start out in an agency where you can learn the ropes by working on a variety of accounts and gain exposure to different businesses—the process of developing a communications strategy is the same, whether you are working on cars or candy. Vicky spent five years in an agency before moving to the client side, and most of her colleagues did the same. "Agency experience is extremely valuable because it exposes you to the bigger picture and involves you in strategic planning and decision making." Packaged goods experience is also valuable in corporate advertising. More and more companies such as service businesses are looking for employees with this background because managing a product at a company like Proctor & Gamble is analogous to running a business, and knowledge of the packaged goods market lays the groundwork for the basics of brand management. When you're starting out, you want the broad-based marketing experience working on different types of products with different target audiences that packaged goods affords, advises Vicky.

But Vicky also believes that managing advertising is about managing people as well as problems, no matter what the

> "During the thirty-six years I've been in the business, I have always been naively guided by the principle that if we do not believe in the products we advertise strongly enough to use them ourselves, we are not completely honest with ourselves in advertising to others."
>
> *–Leo Burnett, founder,*
> *Leo Burnett Company*

Branding has become much more important lately because of the sheer number of choices available to customers. "Technologists tend to think that technology alone will sell their product—that superior technology is the only thing that differentiates them from their competitors," observes Patrick McGovern, chairman of the board of International Data Group, the world's largest computer publishing and research company. [3]

We are clearly in the midst of an information revolution, and computers, technology, and telecommunications are exploding fields desperate for people with marketing skills. If you can tailor your marketing experience and knowledge to these industries, your value as an employee will skyrocket. And since technology is so new and growing so quickly, a little experience in the field can go a long way.

[3]Pettis, Chuck, "The Importance of Brand to The Success of Technology Companies," excerpted from *TechnoBrands: How to Create & Use Brand Identity to Market, Advertise & Sell Technology Products,* AMACOM,1994.

product is. Although any type of advertising, marketing, or business experience is useful—and an MBA certainly can't hurt—a second school of thought on how to break into client-side advertising contends that you can learn how to be a leader and a manager outside of a business atmosphere. Starting in college at the State University of New York in Oswego, Vicky made an effort to skew her experiences toward marketing. She handled publicity and promotion for her sorority, worked in the business division of the student affairs office, and interned with a local Housing and Urban Development center where she wrote promotional materials and brochures. All of these experiences prepared her to work with a team and manage a group effort, which is critical to the advertising process.

Some background in marketing and advertising is important, she says, whether it's a degree, a specialization, or just some course work. But even more important is a well-rounded education that will give you a broader perspective on the world at large. "Advertising is simply an outgrowth of or a response to what's going on in the rest of the world," says Vicky. Advertisers pay close attention to social trends and closely monitor cultural changes to speak meaningfully to consumers. For example, in the 1980s, ads reflected our culture's preoccupation with external displays of status and prestige. But in the past decade there has been "an enormous sea of change in consumer behavior and the things we associate with success have changed," says Nick Utton, MasterCard's senior vice president, U.S. region marketing. Today, having leisure time to enjoy your life and family is more valuable than the label on your pants, and MasterCard has shifted its focus accordingly to reflect society's changing values. Its new campaign breaks away from the materialism that characterized advertising in the 1980s by focusing on the things that money can't buy.

Although writing skills are essential to communicate effectively with customers, they are also necessary to communicate with your company's partner agency. "You are giving the agency direction to help build your business, so it's imperative to be able to clearly explain and justify a point of view. Again, this is a skill you can hone in a variety of areas outside of a business environment," says Vicky.

Professionalism is another key skill to bring to a corporate job, and it's an intangible quality that involves everything from crisis management to the way you answer the phone. These are skills you can begin to learn from summer jobs or internships, and they are skills that you will continue to master throughout your career.

Your ticket into a corporate ad department is a letter and resume to a vice president or director demonstrating that you genuinely care about the business and its products. Show that you are interested in what we do and that you can contribute to our particular business, recommends Vicky. In general, marketing departments are divided into three components: advertising, promotions, and sponsorships. The advertising department consists of a vice president, advertising director, advertising manager, and an advertising coordinator or administrator, the typical entry-level job. Sometimes this position is termed "marketing assistant," and some companies require an MBA at this level. More than likely, you'll start in an administrative capacity with more "executional" or support work, says Vicky. "You *can* learn this way and you *can* get promoted, but don't get stuck at a dead end. Make sure you're part of the larger picture—make sure that after six months or so you have the opportunity for promotion or entrance into a training program."

Although all the creative work is handled by the company's ad agency, many companies have an in-house studio to handle internal projects, and junior writers and art directors can work on annual reports and newsletters. Research also provides many opportunities to work with tracking studies, participate in focus groups, and perform other qualitative and quantitative work while interacting with an ad agency.

Life in a corporate ad department is different from life in an ad agency. Ad agencies thrive on fast-paced, high-energy chaos. "You are always running to meet a deadline and some people thrive on the buzz of nervous energy," Vicky recalls. In a corporate ad environment the stress is of a different variety. An agency reports to its client, meets the client's timetables, and constantly focuses on the client's needs. But as the client you report to the consumer, and the focus shifts to ensuring that your brand is performing, your sales are up, and your customers are happy.

Take a look around an ad agency's creative floor and you're likely to see a lot of young people. Ad agencies are on the cutting edge of pop culture and hip new trends. Agencies are also lean and mean and most people work on several pieces of business, all of which contribute to the frenzied atmosphere. Corporate advertising is much more structured and formal than an ad agency and affords a more balanced lifestyle, says Vicky. "Companies don't want you to burn out and run yourself ragged, whereas this is an expected part of advertising," observes Vicky. "Sure, we have busy periods, but there is also more of an opportunity to have a life outside of work. Our company wants to invest in its employees, because employees who have rich lives bring that richness back to their work."

# PART THREE

## The Keys to Entrance

In any industry there are certain keys that will help you get past the front door. How do you find these keys? How do you ensure that you stay once you've made it in? How do you know which doors to knock on? Read on to discover the answers, the facts, and the contacts.

# *Letters, Resumes, Interviewing, Networking*

## REGINA LEONARD, ASSOCIATE DIRECTOR OF HUMAN RESOURCES
### BBDO Worldwide

In the height of the recruiting season between April and July, BBDO, one of the country's top ten advertising agencies, receives as many as 100 resumes per week. "The reality is that in a calendar year we fill between six and nine entry-level positions in account management and nine to twelve in media," says Regina Leonard, associate director of Human Resources. People average about two years at that level before getting promoted, so job openings are not frequently available.

BBDO fills most of its entry-level jobs by campus recruitment, employee referrals, write-ins, and Job Direct (*see* sidebar). The company occasionally uses employment agencies if it's an off time of year. Word of mouth and networking are also major factors, and Regina encourages college students to use their alumni as a networking tool for informational interviews. Most students don't realize that in the business world, three out of every five jobs are filled by word of mouth, not through recruiters, employment agencies, ads, or by sending letters. That's because 85 percent of job openings are never advertised. Building a network will be the key factor to landing your first job.

Start by compiling a list of people who could potentially know people in advertising, and "courteously exploit" every relationship you have. Begin with your friends and family. Dig out your Christmas card list. Speak to your professors and

## Job Direct

college alumni. (Many schools compile a city-specific list of graduates in various fields specifically for networking purposes.) Talk to people who know a lot of people, such as your clergy, hairdresser, and dentist. And don't be afraid to meet new people. Approach people on the bus who are reading *Ad Age* or *Adweek*. Join business and advertising associations that offer a division for young professionals, mentoring programs, and monthly get-togethers (*see* Appendix for a list of associations in major cities). Most importantly, keep in mind that enthusiasm is infectious and your goal at this stage of the game is to charm someone into giving you 15 minutes of his time.

The best way to get someone interested in you is to express an interest in them: "I saw your fascinating article on your company web site" or "Congratulations on winning the new General Foods account," works wonders as a compliment and conversation opener. Try to leverage some common ground that can establish a personal connection—perhaps you went to the same college, speak the same foreign language, or play the same instrument.

Everyone loves to be a mentor, and people love to talk about themselves. Approach an informational interview armed with questions about your contact, her job, company, and the industry in general: "How did *you* get your first break? What do you love most about advertising? How do you see technology affecting the industry?"

Use each meeting to learn more about the business and walk away with a few more contacts. This is the most effective process for finding a job opening that will never make it to a headhunter or be advertised in the newspaper, so use each informational interview as a rehearsal for the real thing.

Regina also recommends starting the job search process early; if you are a college student start looking in January and February of your senior year. It's more difficult to job hunt if you're not living in the city where you want to work. But, Regina asserts, "if I see someone with an interesting resume I will tell them to call me when they're in New York. I may not have an immediate job opening, but I definitely want to meet the person, and will work around the details if I'm interested in a candidate."

Because jobs are few and far between, Regina looks for someone who shows a dedication to the advertising industry. "Kids are not as starry-eyed about the business as they used to be. Part of the reason may be the quality of life and lack of financial incentive. We still expect killer hours and the money hasn't really changed much over time. You need to sell yourself and convince me that advertising is what you want to do, at least at this point in your life."

Advances in technology have changed the industry; starting out at a large corporate agency no longer affords the same level of prestige. Regina has observed that there is now much more cachet to working with a new media company out of somebody's garage. "Interactive companies have taken on a new dimension and they've stolen the spotlight that advertising once had. Plus, they offer more money, greater opportunity, and a faster growth track. People are flocking to these flat organizations where they can establish a name for themselves and make an impact regardless of their age and experience."

This migration to the new media world creates opportunity for job seekers who can convey their passion for advertising and their desire to be a part of agency life. In addition to dedication, it's important to have a fundamental knowledge of the business and a fairly specific goal. "To avoid turnover, we look for people who are focused. You work long hours for $25,000 and it takes time to feel like you are contributing to the business and making a competitive living. We don't want people who are unprepared for the challenge because they are going to walk away."

To demonstrate your dedication and focus start by writing a cover letter that specifically states what type of position you are seeking. "The opening paragraph has to grab me and tell me exactly why you're writing and what position you're looking for. I don't want to see someone who's on a fishing expedition."

One ad executive recalls a letter he received that went something like this:

> Dear Sir:
>
> I am seeking a corporate position that will allow me to utilize my organizational, administrative, and communication skills in a supportive team-oriented, goal-directed atmosphere where I can contribute to the growth of a company.

Every word of your cover letter will be read (unlike your resume), and this one says absolutely nothing. Your letter must relate personally to the reader, grab his attention, incite his interest, and convince him that you are worth interviewing. Anything else is worthless. An effective cover states the following:

◎ *your objective, directly and clearly*

◎ *direct comparisons between your skills and the company's needs, based on the research you've done about the firm and the industry*

◎ *a date you will call to follow up*

Think of each example in the cover letter as a topic sentence supported with specifics in the resume, advises Rob Sullivan, an advertising recruiter. The cover letter summarizes your experience and relates it to the challenges of the position.[1]

Consider that you are a product and the ad agency, a consumer. Your cover letter and resume is a marketing brief designed to position the strengths of your product and its key selling points. However, your product is still in the development stage. It has rarely been tested; it has not been approved for use. Therefore, you must rely on the product's past performance to indicate how it is capable of performing in the future. Remember, entry-level positions, by definition, are filled by people who have no prior experience. At this level, employers are interested in the "Three Ps": potential, passion, and personality.

◎ Potential. *A resume is not just a summary of your past life, it is a reflection of who you are becoming, says Sullivan. Demonstrate how your past experiences preview what you are capable of doing for an employer in the future by linking your skills and experience to your area of interest. Keep in mind that advertising is not about making ads, it's about selling products and increasing sales; ads just happen to be the most efficient way to accomplish that goal. Tailor your job descriptions appropriately and focus on results. For example, "Organized membership drive for Public Broadcasting System" is less effective than "Organized membership drive for Public Broadcasting System that raised $50,000 and generated a 25% increase in pledges."*

*Advertising is a service business, satisfying the needs of the client day in and day out. If you were involved in any service or retail-oriented business, you can certainly capitalize on your knowledge in this area. You may have also gained invaluable field experience in studying the consumer and learning how to satisfy a customer.*

*Try to think beyond job titles to actual accomplishments. Aside from an internship, most recent college grads have only a smattering of summer jobs to highlight on a resume, and that's to be expected. But you can use those jobs to present a portfolio of skills illustrating your range of attributes and abilities. Think about your jobs from a new perspective; discuss them with a friend, teacher, or advisor. This discussion often can help you to draw out some unique knowledge*

[1]Sullivan, Rob, *Climbing Your Way to The Bottom*, Play Publishing, Chicago, Il, 1996, p. 26.

*you gained from your work. A summer lifeguarding job, for example, can be used to demonstrate leadership, responsibility, problem-solving, and organizational skills, along with the ability to work with a team.*

◎ Passion. *Nearly every person interviewed for this book made reference to the fact that passion and a burning drive to succeed in advertising are critical to breaking in and succeeding in the business. Although your resume needs to support your goals, it simultaneously needs to communicate this "fire in your belly" by showing that you have the motivation and initiative to tackle new challenges. Regina stresses that if you complete an internship it can certainly play to your advantage by shaping your focus; however, BBDO has certainly hired people who have not interned but were involved in entrepreneurial ventures. Starting your own school club, for example, demonstrates leadership and creativity.*

◎ Personality. *Charisma, energy, and personality are just as important, if not more so, at this stage of the game. What makes you unique? How do your experiences and interests define you as a person? Personalizing your resume is key to making it stand out from the crowd. Use unique and specific details that set you apart from other people, both in your jobs and interests. "We look for a well-developed person, culturally well-rounded with lots of interests. A lot of people seeking a position in account management have no clue about what's going on out in the world, not the latest current event—nothing. An applicant with a basic marketing degree who has followed the standard path often lacks this broader perspective and isn't somebody who breaks out of the mold. I look for someone with a liberal arts degree who's had some business coursework, but I put a lot more weight into the overall package."*

> **❝ Be a Renaissance person. You have to have a life outside advertising. You have to know what's going on and be aware of what's happening. Because if you don't have a life outside, you don't have anything to bring to the job."**
>
> **–Tom Burell, founder, Burell Communications**

*Some people read a resume from the bottom up,*

*beginning with your interests. If photography is one of your hobbies, what type do you enjoy? Landscape photography, pet photography? Some job candidates report that as many as 80 percent of questions generated by the resume result from the interviewer identifying with a similar area of interest.*

BBDO generally hires college grads into assistant account executive (AAE) or assistant media positions as opposed to strictly secretarial jobs. Although this is not standard for the industry, the company believes that if you want an AAE job and interview for that position, they will evaluate you against the criteria for that position. "If I don't hire someone as an AAE, chances are I'm not hiring them for anything else," says Regina. "We don't encourage hiring college grads into administrative positions because we don't want the constant turnover. There have definitely been case histories of people who were secretaries and climbed the ranks. But in today's market I would hold out. It depends on the company—if the agency has a history of taking college grads into administrative jobs, which can serve as a springboard into a promotable career track position after a year, then I would consider it. But we don't bring people in at this level with that intention. We don't say that it won't happen, but we don't position it as an option."

BBDO doesn't just stick to recent college grads to fill entry-level positions—they also employ people who are making career changes. "We definitely hire a mix of people, some of whom have been out in the world for a year or so. We recently hired someone who had gone back to school for his Master's, had a unique internship in sports marketing, and an interesting undergrad background. He was smart, met all the criteria for an account management position, and was hired because of his broad experience across the board."

BBDO looks for the same attributes that most companies seek in an entry-level employee, irrespective of the industry: someone who is thought-provoking, articulate, has a strong presence, and shows interest and excitement during the interview. "We like people who can demonstrate that they are creative thinkers, that they have an appreciation for creativity, along with a fundamental knowledge of advertising. They should be able to articulate why it is they're interested in a particular position, and correlate their experience with that interest." Regina will use prospects' resumes to try to unearth their

> "I try to draw the person out, beginning with high school years. I want to find out if he or she played sports, was involved in politics, or what his or her folks do. I try to find out what kind of a person he or she is."
>
> —*Stan Richards, founder, The Richards Group*

leadership skills, communication skills, and ability to think creatively. "If you were on a sports team, be prepared to explain how you motivated people and how you lead your team to success."

Preparation is key to a successful interview. Research the agency, read up on some of the trade magazines, and have a general sense of what's going on in the industry. People use the same lines over and over, says Regina. "Don't tell me you want to get into advertising because you love to work with people, or because you love commercials," she warns. "At the same time, don't tell me you never watch commercials because you don't have time for television. Be able to tell me about your favorite advertisement or how you would change an ad to improve it."

Be prepared to encounter one of three major types of interviewing styles:

◎ The Behavioral Interview. *This interview is based on the assumption that your past work is predictive of your future performance, and the interviewer will ask you to describe work situations, problems, and solutions. The best tactic to use in this situation is the* **STAR** *technique.*

*Situation: Describe your circumstances and the nature of your job.*

*Task: Talk about your assignment.*

*Action: Review the plan you created and the steps you took to resolution.*

*Results: Emphasize and quantify, if possible, the outcome of your actions.*

◎ The Analytical Interview. *This technique investigates how you solve problems, think on your feet, and perform under pressure. The interviewer is interested in your thinking process rather than an exact answer. Questions could include, "How many escalators are there in New York?" or "Sell me this paper clip." An interviewer may also challenge you with a stressful situation to see how you react. One candidate tells the story of entering the office to find the interviewer leaning back in his chair, feet on the desk, engrossed in a newspaper article. "Get my attention," he challenged. (The brazen young applicant took out his lighter and set the paper on fire.)*

◎ The Manhattan, Kansas, Interview. *Here, the interviewer is thinking, "If I was stuck in an airport in Manhattan, Kansas, would I want to be stuck with this candidate?" This is where your personality has to shine, and you need to demonstrate that you are a fun, exciting, and interesting person.* [2]

Although ad agencies are not as "corporate" as other businesses, the interview is still a formal process. "Some people sit very casually, very laid-back, others lean on their elbows on my desk." Sit straight, "on the edge of your seat" to convey attention and enthusiasm. Don't be so aggressive that you're jumping across the desk but at the same time you can't be too meek as if you're hiding in the corner. "I get a lot of people who are very monotone and just kind of sit there," says Regina. "At the same time I see a lot of people who are overly arrogant and think they're ready to run the company. Everyone wants to come in and create his or her own job and earn $100,000. They have a certain level of arrogance and expectation, and this needs to be balanced with a healthy sense of humility."

If you can't land that first job in advertising, by all means go out and do something related, recommends Regina. Go into ad sales or work as an administrative coordinator in a marketing department. Do something unique or something else professional in another capacity, and try it again in another year. Regina took this same advice herself. She wanted a job in account management at Saatchi & Saatchi, but back in the late 1980s they were only hiring individuals with MBAs, so they offered her a position in human resources instead. "I was heartbroken but I took the job having no idea what I was getting into. As a result, I was exposed to an area I never would have dreamed about as a career, and I stayed in human resources because I found it well suited to my skills and capabilities and very rewarding. So I never ask those questions about what you want to do in five years."

"I tell a lot of people that your first job isn't always going to be the perfect job. It should be a career path you want to pursue and a job that you should have an interest in, at least as a hobby, but it's a job where you will learn about yourself outside the academic world. You need to grow and mature, learn about your likes and dislikes, strengths and weaknesses."

"You need to go into that job, if it's not the ideal job, and take every experience for what it's worth and make the most of it without belittling or begrudging it, because a lot of times you can make something of it even if you never thought you could. It's a balance between having a focus but also being willing to try something different if the opportunity comes along."

[2]Sanborn, Bob and Lederman, Eva, *How to Get a Job in New York City*, Surry Books, Chicago, IL. 1998, pp.174-177.

# U.S. Ad Agencies, Associations, and Recruiters

## AGENCIES—ATLANTA

### ADAIR GREENE ADVERTISING

200 Atlanta Tech. Ctr.
1575 Northside Dr.
Atlanta, GA 30318
404-351-8424
404-351-1495 (fax)

**Employees:** 120
**Annual billings:** $24,000,000
**Number of entry-level positions:** 30 (in growth spurt)
**Job types:** Traffic, primarily in healthcare division
**Average starting salary:** $18,000
**Overtime:** No
**Training program:** No
**Internships:** Open to interns as agency grows
**Number of interns:** None in the past
**Internship contact:** Janet Powell
**Personnel contact:** Same

### AFA SERVICE CORPORATION

11 Piedmont Ctr., Ste. 720
Atlanta, GA 30305
404-262-2729
404-262-2731 (fax)

**Employees:** 50
**Annual billings:** $14,000,000
**Number of entry-level positions:** 3
**Job types:** Data administrator, administrative assistant, production manager
**Average starting salary:** $23,000
**Overtime:** yes
**Training program:** In all departments
**Internships:** No
**Personnel contact:** Cheryl Caudy, Office Manager and Human Resources

### AUSTIN KELLEY ADVERTISING

5901 Peachtree Dunwoody Rd., NE
Atlanta, GA 30328
770-396-6666
770-396-0301 (fax)

**Employees:** 83
**Annual billings:** $85,000,000
**Number of entry-level positions:** 5

**Job types:** Account coordinator, assistant media planner/buyer, reception
**Average starting salary:** $18,000–$20,000
**Overtime:** yes
**Training program:** No
**Internships:** In media and account service during summer; paid minimum wage
**Number of interns:** 2
**Internship contact:** Maria Beasley; maria@austinkelley.com
**Personnel contact:** Same

### AYDLOTTE & CARTWRIGHT

Six Concourse Pkwy., Ste. 2800
Atlanta, GA 30328
770-551-5000
770-551-5001 (fax)

**Employees:** 38
**Annual billings:** $28,000,000
**Number of entry-level positions:** 4
**Job types:** Account coordinator
**Average starting salary:** NA
**Training program:** No
**Internships:** 90-day rotation in different departments; unpaid
**Number of interns:** 3
**Internship contact:** Lynne Gregory
**Personnel contact:** Same

### BBDO SOUTH

1600 Monarch Pl., 3414 Peachtree Rd., NE
Atlanta, GA 30326
404-231-1700
404-841-1671 (fax)

**Employees:** 45
**Annual billings:** $5,634,000,000 (worldwide)
**Number of entry-level positions:** 30
**Job types:** Account management, media
**Average starting salary:** $17,500–$24,000
**Overtime:** No
**Training program:** Media, account services; hosts media school within department and BBDO seminars
**Internships:** Media, account services; year-round; paid
**Number of interns:** 20
**Internship contact:** Wendy Vogelman; wvogelman@bbdoatl.com

**Personnel contact:** Debbie Powell, senior vice president, human resources director

## COLE HENDERSON DRAKE

426 Marietta St.
Atlanta, GA 30313
404-892-4500
404-892-4522 (fax)

**Employees:** 35
**Annual billings:** $26,900,000
**Number of entry-level positions:** NA
**Job types:** Account service, administrative
**Average starting salary:** $20,000–$25,000
**Overtime:** No
**Training program:** No
**Internships:** Account service and media during the summer; unpaid
**Number of interns:** 4
**Internship contact:** Bob White
**Personnel contact:** Same

## DONINO & PARTNERS

7000 Central Pkwy., Ste. 1350
Atlanta, GA 30328
770-668-5700
770-668-5707 (fax)
www.donino.com

**Employees:** 36
**Annual billings:** $17,500,000
**Number of entry-level positions:** 5
**Job types:** Account coordinator, media assistant
**Average starting salary:** $21,000
**Overtime:** Yes
**Training program:** No
**Internships:** Year-round in all departments, depending on need; many in account services; paid $8/hr.
**Number of interns:** 2
**Internship contact:** Susan Hasewinkle; susan@donino.com
**Personnel contact:** Same

## FITZGERALD & CO.

One Buckhead Plaza
3060 Peachtree Rd., NW, Ste. 500
Atlanta, GA 30305
404-262-8900
404-239-0548 (fax)

**Employees:** 78
**Annual billings:** $548,000,000
**Number of entry-level positions:** 2–3
**Job types:** NA
**Average starting salary:** NA
**Training program:** No
**Internships:** From time to time, depending on departmental needs; paid
**Number of interns:** NA
**Internship contact:** Linda Kobel
**Personnel contact:** Same

## FRICKS ADVERTISING

Six Concourse Pkwy., Ste. 3300
Atlanta, GA 30328
770-396-6206
770-396-0207 (fax)

**Employees:** 30
**Annual billings:** $31,000,000
**Number of entry-level positions:** 3
**Job types:** Account services, creative
**Average starting salary:** NA
**Training program:** No
**Internships:** Year-round in all departments; paid
**Number of interns:** 2
**Internship contact:** Shirley Harris; fricksad@mindspring.com
**Personnel contact:** Same

## FREEBAIRN & CO.

3343 Peachtree Rd., Ste. 1220
Atlanta, GA 30326
404-237-9945
404-231-2214 (fax)
www.freebairn.com

**Employees:** 60
**Annual billings:** $18,500,000
**Number of entry-level positions:** 3
**Job types:** Assistant media planner, account coordinator, receptionist

**Average starting salary:** $18,000
**Overtime:** No
**Training program:** No
**Internships:** Year-round in account services, media, maybe PR; paid
**Number of interns:** 2
**Internship contact:** Jean G. Cobb, vice president, account supervisor; jeanc@freebairn.com
**Personnel contact:** Toni Cooper, SVE, controller/finance; tonic@freebairn.com

## GOLIN/HARRIS COMMUNICATIONS

50 Hurt Plaza
Atlanta, GA 30303
404-681-3808
404-681-9029 (fax)
www.golinharris.com

**Employees:** 15
**Annual billings:** NA
**Number of entry-level positions:** 4
**Job types:** Assistant account executive, account coordinator
**Average starting salary:** $22,000
**Overtime:** No
**Training program:** Client services, marketing
**Internships:** Quarterly in client services, marketing
**Number of interns:** 8
**Internship contact:** Deirdre Alexander; dalexander@golinharris.com
**Personnel contact:** Malik Watler, office administrator; mwatler@golinharris.com

## T.G. MADISON

3340 Peachtree Rd. NE, Ste. 2850
Atlanta, GA 30326
404-262-2623
404-237-2811 (fax)

**Employees:** 35
**Annual billings:** $16,000,000
**Number of entry-level positions:** 5
**Job types:** Assistant account executive, account coordinator, new business coordinator, junior Mac artist, proofreader
**Average starting salary:** NA
**Overtime:** No
**Training program:** Account service
**Internships:** Spring, summer, and fall in account service, finance

**Number of interns:** 2
**Internship contact:** Janelle Erwin; jerwin@dscga.com
**Personnel contact:** Same

## MCCANN-ERICKSON/ATLANTA

615 Peachtree NE
Atlanta, GA 30365
404-881-3100
404-881-3128 (fax)

**Employees:** 100
**Annual billings:** $7,178,000,000 (worldwide)
**Number of entry-level positions:** 12
**Job types:** Assistant account executive, assistant media planner/buyer, junior accounting executive
**Average starting salary:** NA
**Training program:** No
**Internships:** Periodically in all departments, depending on workload; paid
**Number of interns:** 4
**Internship contact:** Kirk Thompson
**Personnel contact:** Each department handles own personnel

## POLLAK LEVITT CHAIET ADVERTISING

One Piedmont Center, Ste. 505
Atlanta, GA 30305
404-261-1566
404-261-2029 (fax)
www.plcatlanta.com

**Employees:** 40
**Annual billings:** $29,000,000
**Number of entry-level positions:** 3
**Job types:** Media assistant, account coordinator
**Average starting salary:** $20,000
**Overtime:** Yes
**Training program:** No
**Internships:** Year-round in account services, creative, media; paid
**Number of interns:** 4
**Internship contact:** James S. Pollack; pollack@plcatlanta.com
**Personnel contact:** Jill Austin; austin@plcatlanta.com

## OGILVY & MATHER

75 14th St., Ste. 3000
Atlanta, GA 30309
404-888-5100
404-888-5147 (fax)

**Employees:** 60
**Annual billings:** $ 7,600,000,000 (worldwide)
**Number of entry-level positions:** NA
**Job types:** Media, account services, research, direct mail
**Average starting salary:** NA
**Training program:** No
**Internships:** Available in all departments during summer; paid
**Number of interns:** NA
**Internship contact:** Tracy Merry; tracy.merry@ogilvy.com
**Personnel contact:** Same

## SAWYER RILEY COMPTON

1100 Abernathy Rd., Ste. 800
Atlanta, GA 30328
404-479-9849
404-393-9953 (fax)

**Employees:** 45
**Annual billings:** $50,000,000
**Number of entry-level positions:** 2
**Job types:** Junior public relations, accounts payable; generally don't fill entry-level spots in ad departments
**Training program:** No
**Internships:** Year-round in PR, account management
**Number of interns:** 4
**Internship contact:** Connie Reeves; connie@src-online.com
**Personnel contact:** Same

## WESTERN INTERNATIONAL MEDIA CORPORATION

7 Piedmont Center, Ste. 300
Atlanta, GA 30305
404-814-8711
404-239-0593 (fax)
www.wimc.com

**Employees:** 150
**Annual billings:** $2,395,000,000

**Number of entry-level positions:** 50
**Job types:** Media assistants, billing assistants, print buying assistants, administrative assistants, receptionists, clerks
**Average starting salary:** $18,000–$21,000
**Overtime:** No
**Training program:** Media, billing, print
**Internships:** Looking into developing a program in account services
**Number of interns:** 1
**Internship contact:** Lynne Baker; lynneb@wimc.com
**Personnel contact:** David Strauss, senior vice president, director of client services; davidst@wimc.com

Gail Scott, executive vice president, regional media director; gailst@wimc.com

# ATLANTA—ASSOCIATIONS

## LINKS TO ADVERTISING AGENCIES IN ATLANTA

www.telefilm-south.com/Georgia/CI/adagencies.html

## LINKS TO ADVERTISING/COMMUNICATION ASSOCIATIONS IN ATLANTA

www.telefilm-south.com/Georgia/Oz/assoc.shtml

## AMERICAN MARKETING ASSOCIATION

1706 NE Expressway
Atlanta, GA 30329
770-235-3500, ext 128
AMA Hotline: 404-222-2779

The AMA's Atlanta chapter offers a wide variety of programs and dozens of special interest seminars and workshops throughout the year for everyone involved in or considering the marketing profession, whether at the senior management or college level. Monthly luncheons are held the second Thursday of each month at 11:30 a.m.; call the AMA Hotline for location and speaker information.

## ATLANTA ADVERTISING CLUB

P.O. Box 500846
Atlanta, GA 31150
770-649-8872

The Atlanta Ad Club is the primary organization for Atlanta advertising professionals, representing all segments of the advertising community. The Club offers a variety of educational opportunities, including Evening at Emory, Career Day, seminars and workshops. Meetings are generally the third Tuesday of each month.

## AD/2 ATLANTA

3340 Peachtree Rd.
Atlanta, GA
404-264-6223

Ad/2 Atlanta is a non-profit organization of young advertising, public relations, marketing, and communication professionals who meet to further their business education and obtain hands-on experience. The group meets the third Tuesday of each month at the Wyndham Garden Hotel on Peachtree Road next to Tower Place. Networking and cocktails begin at 6 p.m., speaker at 7 p.m. Meetings are free to members and $10.00 for guests.

## BUSINESS MARKETING ASSOCIATION

c/o 3654 Cherbourg Way
Marietta, GA 30062
770-971-5898
BMA Information Line: 770-322-2188
Contact: Pat Semmelmayer

Business Marketing Association (BMA) is a business-to-business organization consisting of professionals in marketing, advertising, production, promotion, and public relations. BMA holds monthly meetings where members and guests can network and learn about the marketing industry from top professionals. The meetings are held the first Thursday of every month at 103 West on West Paces Ferry Road in Buckhead. The cost is $28.00

for members and $35.00 for nonmembers; call 770-322-2188 for reservations. Other benefits include a newsletter, member directory, access to conferences and seminars, reciprocal membership in BPA International, and discounts on a variety of products and services. BMA members can also earn the Certified Business Communicator certificate, a unique credential that demonstrates competence in the field of business-to-business marketing communications.

## THE PORTFOLIO CENTER

125 Bennett St. NW
Atlanta, GA 30309
404-351-5055
800-255-3169
www.portfoliocenter.com

The Portfolio Center is a prestigious and highly competitive school for copywriting, art direction, illustration, photography and graphic design. Every industry expert has taught a class or lead a seminar at the Portolio Center, from Bill Westbrook and Jay Chiat to Dan Wieden and Kerry Casey.

"The single most important thing you will learn at every turn in your career here is this: How to think. Because at Portfolio Center, concept is king. Ideas rule. You will learn strategy, positioning, and target identification. You will learn supers, one-shots, voiceovers, spreads and taglines. You will learn the critical importance of the idea. The idea is, after all, the difference between eloquence and persuasion," according to the Portfolio Center. But you will also learn "the pure business skills you need to be competitive. Clients. Budgets. Timelines. Production. Politics. How to present your own work. How to start and sustain a business. How to ask for a raise...that's what Portfolio Center is all about."

## THE CREATIVE CIRCUS

1935 Cliff Valley Way, Ste. 210
Atlanta, GA 30329
404-633-1990
www.collegeedge.com/details/college/1/7/
d4_3707

Atlanta is known for training and producing top-notch creatives, and many come out of the Creative Circus. In fact, the school boasts an 87 percent placement rate for students who enter jobs within two years of graduation.

## THE CREATIVE CLUB OF ATLANTA

807 W. Marietta, Studio M204
Atlanta, GA 30318
404-874-0908
www.creativeclub.org

The Creative Club of Atlanta is comprised of professionals from all areas of advertising and design, as well as students pursuing careers in those fields. Cost for monthly programs is $5.00 for members and $25.00 for nonmembers. Memberships are available at a special rate for young professionals and students and include a membership directory, newsletter, and discounts on all programs and entry fees.

## DIRECT MARKETING ASSOCIATION (DMA), ATLANTA CHAPTER

229 Peachtree Street, Ste. 960
Atlanta, GA 30303
404-681-3622

DMA members include 3,600 member companies from the United States and 49 other nations, as well as direct marketers from every business segment including non-profit and electronic marketing. DMA members receive access to the DMA Library & Resource Center's DirectLINK reference database of direct marketing information; subscriptions to leading DMA publications, including *Washington Report, Direct Line, Annual Report* and *The DMA Insider*; and listings in the DMA Membership Directory.

## FREELANCE FORUM

P.O. Box 250024
Atlanta, GA 30325
404-705-2400

The Freelance Forum is comprised of more than 100 creative/art directors, graphic designers, desktop publishers, illustrators, writers, photographers and multimedia artists, and producers. Membership includes monthly meetings with featured speakers, exposure to potential clients through the annual directory and Portfolio Show, and business discounts. Meetings are held the first Thursday of each month. Meetings are free for members and $7.00 for nonmembers. Membership dues are $65.00/year, $50.00/year for students.

## THE INTERACTIVE MEDIA ALLIANCE

GCATT Building
250 14th Street, NW
Fourth Floor
Atlanta, GA 30318
www.tima.org

TIMA promotes leadership of interactive media technology and acts as a forum for networking, job hunting, and exchanging techniques and tools. Meetings are held the second Thursday of each month (excluding August and December) and feature organized presentations by leaders in the interactive media industry. Members are also eligible for medical insurance and public relations assistance. Membership is $125.00 for individuals.

## INTERNATIONAL INTERACTIVE COMMUNICATIONS SOCIETY

404-264-4427
www.iics.org

As the primary resource in Georgia for anyone interested in multimedia and interactivity, this group includes professionals from all areas of multimedia who come together to share their knowledge and expertise. Open to everyone who wants to enhance their multimedia careers. Meetings, held at the Georgia Center for Advanced Telecommunications Technology, are free for members and $10.00 for guests.

## RECRUITERS—ATLANTA

### WORK

2870 Peachtree Rd, Ste. 110
Atlanta, GA 30305
404-681-5656
www. workonline.net
Rickm@ workonline.net
Contact: Rick Myers

Work places recent college grads directly out of school in all types of entry-level advertising positions around the country. The companies have between 50 and 75 clients, from large agencies to small boutiques and media shops such as Western International Media. "We can place a young person in a position anywhere in the country" says Rick, a recruiter, "if they are eager, enthusiastic and willing to learn. A high grade point average doesn't hurt either. Nor does an academic background in advertising, marketing, public relations, communications, or related studies. There has been a crunch for talent in the past few years and there are lots of jobs open." But at the same time Rick admits that "creatively, Atlanta is a little defunct. We need more creative and account personnel. It's not a good advertising town right now. The West coast is a much better place for a young person to start out."

Work also publishes free guides on interviewing and resume writing for advertising.

### ASK GUY TUCKER, INC.

4990 High Point Road
Atlanta, GA 30342
404-303-7177
www.askguy.com
guy@askguy.com

Ask Guy Tucker, Inc., is an Atlanta-based resource company specializing in advertising

headhunting and recruitment, interactive multimedia services, and television commercial film production. "Most agencies can find younger folks on their own, but when they ask me I am pleased to help. Because I work closely with the Portfolio Center and the Creative Circus (and often find teachers and lecturers for them), I have a good feel for the market for recent graduates,"says Guy.

## AGENICES—BOSTON

### ARNOLD COMMUNICATIONS

101 Arch St.
Boston, MA 02110
617-737-6400
617-737-6658 (fax)
www.ar.com

**Employees:** 735
**Annual billings:** $512,000,000
**Number of entry-level positions:** NA
**Job types:** Account coordinator, media planner, assistant art director, traffic assistant, administrative assistant, receptionist
**Average starting salary:** $20,000–$23,000
**Overtime:** Yes
**Training program:** No
**Internships:** Fall, spring, summer, in creative, account management, broadcast, direct, sports marketing, PR; all unpaid
**Number of interns:** NA
**Internship contact:** Anita Lamoureux
**Personnel contact:** Same

### BERENSON, ISHAM & PARTNERS

31 Milk St.
Boston, MA 02109
617-423-1120
617-423-4597(fax)
www.bipi.com

**Employees:** 18
**Annual billings:** NA
**Number of entry level positions:** 3
**Job types:** Account coordinator, administrative assistant, intern
**Average starting salary:** $22,000
**Overtime:** Yes
**Training program:** Account management

**Internships:** Account management; paid
**Number of interns:** 2
**Internship contact:** Diana Lanham; dlanham@bipi.com, 617-210-1128
**Personnel contact:** Same

## BRONNER SLOSBERG HUMPHREY

The Prudential Tower
800 Boylston St.
Boston, MA 02199
617-867-1000
617-867-1111 (fax)

**Employees:** 800
**Annual billings:** $525,000,000
**Number of entry-level positions:** NA
**Job types:** Account management, traffic, media, finance
**Average starting salary:** NA
**Training program:** All new employees participate in 3-month training process, electing different areas of interest
**Internships:** Depending on need, irregular, random program during summer
**Number of interns:** Handful
**Internship contact:** Susan Moller
**Personnel contact:** Same

## CLARKE GOWARD

535 Boylston St.
Boston, MA 02116
617-536-7611
617-536-4288 (fax)
www.clarkegoward.com

**Employees:** 29
**Annual billings:** $29,000,000
**Number of entry-level positions:** 0
**Job types:** Traffic, account management, administrative
**Average starting salary:** NA
**Internships:** Year-round in all departments; paid and unpaid
**Number of interns:** 6-8
**Internship contact:** Diane Lawson; dlawson@clarkegoward.com
**Personnel contact:** Same

## GREENBERG SERONICK & PARTNERS

855 Boylston St.
Boston, MA 02116
617-267-4949
617-267-7322 (fax)
www.gsop.com

**Employees:** 30
**Annual billings:** $34,750,000
**Number of entry-level positions:** 5
**Job types:** Assistant account executive, assistant media planner, media analyst, mac designer, receptionist
**Average starting salary:** $18,000–$22,000
**Overtime:** No
**Training program:** Account services, media
**Internships:** Year-round in account services, creative, public relations; paid and unpaid
**Number of interns:** 5
**Internship contact:** Melanie Mowdy, account supervisor
**Personnel contact:** Jim Rowean, director of account services

## HILL, HOLLIDAY, CONNORS, COSMOPULOS

John Hancock Tower
200 Clarendon St.
Boston, MA 02116
617-437-1600
617-572-3534 (fax)
www.hhcc.com

**Employees:** 500
**Annual billings:** $281,556,000
**Number of entry-level positions:** 40
**Job types:** Various
**Average starting salary:** NA
**Overtime:** For certain positions
**Training program:** In various departments
**Internships:** Fall, spring, summer, in all departments; only summer is paid
**Number of interns:** 100
**Internship contact:** Jackie Lynam 617-859-4412/JLynam@hhcc.com
**Personnel contact:** Same

## HOUSTON HERSTEK FAVAT

360 Newbury St.
Boston, MA 02115
617-375-7200
617-267-6472 (fax)
www.houston.com

**Employees:** 60
**Annual billings:** $168,648,000
**Number of entry-level positions:** NA
**Average starting salary:** Low $20s
**Overtime:** Yes
**Training program:** Training for internal employees in all departments
**Internships:** Summer and each semester in all departments; paid
**Number of interns:** 10/semester and 15/summer
**Internship contact:** Lisa Johnson; lj@hema.com
**Personnel contact:** Same

## INGALLS, QUINN & JOHNSON

855 Boylston St.
Boston, MA 02116
617-295-7000
617-295-7514 (fax)
www.ingallsboston.com

**Employees:** 175
**Annual billings:** $108,450,000
**Number of entry-level positions:** 15
**Job types:** Account coordinator, administrative assistant
**Average starting salary:** $20,500
**Overtime:** Yes
**Training program:** Internal
**Internships:** In every department during spring, fall and summer; credit only
**Number of interns:** 18–25
**Internship contact:** Kristin Grace
**Personnel contact:** Rebecca Sullivan

## KELLEY DEXTER

160 Federal St.
Boston, MA 02110
617-946-0606
617-946-0909 (fax)

**Employees:** 20
**Annual billings:** NA

**Number of entry level positions:** 2
**Job types:** Account management, creative
**Average starting salary:** $20,000–25,000
**Overtime:** No
**Training program:** No
**Internships:** Year-round in account management and creative; unpaid
**Number of interns:** 2
**Internship contact:** Lee Gustafson; lgustafson@kelleydexter.com
**Personnel contact:** Same

## KELLEY HABIB JOHN INTEGRATED MARKETING

One Constitution Plaza
Boston, MA 02129-2025
617-241-8000
617-241-8110 (fax)
www.khj.com

**Employees:** 45
**Annual billings:** $24,000,000
**Number of entry-level positions:** 5
**Job types:** Production coordinator, account services coordinator, public relations coordinator
**Average starting salary:** $25,000–$30,000
**Overtime:** No
**Training program:** No
**Internships:** Year-round, in public relations, account service, business development, creative; paid and unpaid
**Number of interns:** 4
**Internship contact:** Lynda Butler; lbutler@khj.com
**Personnel contact:** Same

## LEHMAN MILLET

280 Summer St.
Boston, MA 02210
617-439-0288
617-634-0323 (fax)
www.lminc.com

**Employees:** 48
**Annual Billings:** $32,000,000
**Entry-level Positions:** 6
**Job types:** Account coordinator, administrative assistant, receptionist
**Average starting salary:** $22,000
**Overtime:** No
**Training program:** No

**Internships:** On an as-needed basis in account services, research, design, PR; none in media; paid
**Number of interns:** 1
**Internship contact:** Irene Donovan; irene_donovan@millet.com
**Personnel contact:** Same

## PAGANO, SCHENCK & KAY

420 Boylston St.
Boston, MA 02116
617-859-5757
617-262-7703 (fax)
www.psk.com

**Employees:** 25
**Annual billings:** $36,000,000
**Number of entry-level positions:** 2
**Job types:** Media
**Average starting salary:** $18,000–$20,000
**Overtime:** No
**Training program:** No
**Internships:** In all departments throughout the year; paid
**Number of interns:** 6
**Internship contact:** Joann Nelson; jnelson@psk.com
**Personnel contact:** Same

## PARRISH WICKERSHAM & PARTNERS (SUBSIDIARY OF ARNOLD)

The Berkley Building
420 Boylston St.
Boston, MA 02116
617-424-0300
617-424-0399 (fax)

**Employees:** 65
**Annual billings:** $80,000,000
**Personnel contact:** Susan Roche

## TRINITY COMMUNICATIONS

399 Boylston St.
Boston, MA 02166
617-578-6034
617-578-1440 (fax)
www.trinitynet.com

**Employees:** 49
**Annual billings:** $35,000,000
**Number of entry-level positions:** 6
**Job types:** Junior positions in creative and account services; agency does not have job titles
**Average starting salary:** NA
**Training program:** On-the-job training; junior person is paired with a senior mentor
**Internships:** College students and recent grads are accepted to summer and year-round paid program that averages 6 months; students work with a team of employees, and 70–80 percent of hires come from intern program.
**Number of interns:** 8–10 at all times
**Internship contact:** Steven Wallace; tci@trinity.com
**Personnel contact:** Same

## WALLWORK CURRY

181 Newberry St.
Boston, MA 02116
617-266-8200
617-266-8270 (fax)
www.wcadv.com

**Employees:** 25
**Annual billings:** $25,000,000
**Number of entry-level positions:** 4
**Job types:** Account service, media, art studio, reception
**Average starting salary:** NA
**Training program:** No
**Internships:** Year-round in all departments; unpaid
**Number of interns:** 6–7
**Internship contact:** Alison Atanasio; alison@wcadv.com
**Personnel contact:** Same

# BOSTON—ASSOCIATIONS

## THE ADVERTISING CLUB OF GREATER BOSTON

38 Newberry St.
Boston, MA 02116
617-262-1100
www.adclub.org

Events include interactive marketing day, monthly "drop-in" social, four portfolio reviews per year, and an annual career conference. The Club offers continuing education courses taught by top professionals in the advertising field. The three course areas are creative concepts, marketing and communications, and learning exchange sessions; marketing classes include Introduction to Advertising and Marketing, Direct Marketing, the Web as a Marketing Tool, and Overview of Media Strategies.

## AMERICAN MARKETING ASSOCIATION, BOSTON CHAPTER

95 Lura Lane
Waltham, MA 02154
781-237-9511
www.ama.org
Contact: Suzanne Roy
(see description under Chicago listing)

## THE MASSACHUSETTS INTERACTIVE MEDIA COUNCIL

43 Charles Street
Boston, MA 02114
617-227-2822
www.mimc.org

MIMC supports the interactive industry in Massachusetts and includes the area's leading creative talent in new media as well as up-and-coming hopefuls. At MIMC's nearly 70 annual events, the group tackles creative as well as business topics that prove to be educational and sometimes controversial. Networking is a large part of MIMC forums and "sometimes we just drink beer and socialize."

MIMC benefits include a job bank, discounted training seminars and an interactive conference weekend. Membership for full-time students is $25.00/year.

## NEW ENGLAND DIRECT MARKETING ASSOCIATION

6 Abbott Road
Wellesley Hills, MA 02181
781-237-1366
www.nedma.com

At NEDMA's monthly events, you'll learn more about every aspect of direct marketing—creative, strategy, lists, media, telemarketing, database techniques, production, and more. Monthly meetings, which begin with a networking and social hour, feature local direct-marketing pros who share their knowledge.

NEDMA's major event is the annual Spring Conference, which offers an in-depth look at the dynamics of direct marketing and features guest speakers, panel discussions, critiques, sessions for novices and experts, exhibits, and an annual awards presentation.

Member benefits include a complete and up-to-date listing of ad agencies and direct marketing services in New England, a 20 percent discount on Bentley College's Direct Marketing Certificate Program, an independent professional development program; the NEDMA newsletter with news and tips on direct marketing; free admission to the Paul Butterworth Seminar, an annual free seminar that features expert direct marketers offering advice on the art of copywriting.

Annual dues are $160.00 per person and include a free subscription to *Direct Marketing Magazine*.

# RECRUITERS—BOSTON

## ADVANCE

A Division of Robert Half International
60 Mall Rd.
Burlington, MA 01803
781-273-4250

Advance specializes in creative communications including graphic design, multimedia, and web development. The firm places candidates in traffic, production management, and assistant account executive positions, and it reviews creative portfolios. "We look for people with entry-level experience, such as an internship," says David Penn, office services manager. "Strong computer skills are essential, as is a strong desire to learn new software packages," he recommends. "Young job seekers should have a sense of how much they need to learn."

Arnold and Ingalls are the only two large agencies still in Boston and there are no medium-sized shops left, notes Penn. This is a good time to look for a job in Boston and it is easier to break into a small shop. Since unemployment is low, there are lots of long-term temp hires, so don't be afraid to take a two- or three-month position if you haven't found the right full-time job, he advises.

## CHALONER

PO Box 1097, Back Bay Station
Boston, 20117
617-451-5170
Contact: Ted Chaloner, President

Specializes in communications jobs with both agencies and corporations. Places candidates with at least 1–2 years experience in advertising, marketing, public relations, and corporate communications.

## FARRINGTON ASSOCIATES

200 Clarendon St., 40th Fl.
Boston, MA 02116
617-859-4188

Nancy Farrington considers people with a minimum of four years experience for positions such as planners and account executives. Her advice to recent college grads: "Look into the smaller up-and-coming agencies in Boston and contact their presidents directly."

# AGENCIES — CHICAGO

## A. EICOFF & CO.

401 N. Michigan Ave., Ste. 400
Chicago, IL 60611
312-527-7100
312-527-7179 (fax)

**Employees:** 90
**Annual billings:** $80,979,000
**Number of entry-level positions:** 8
**Job types:** Media assistant, assistant account executive, junior copywriter, clerical

**Average starting salary:** Low $20s, assistant account executives slightly higher
**Overtime:** No
**Training program:** No
**Internships:** Client services during summer; paid
**Number of interns:** 2
**Internship contact:** Cathy Watt; cathy.watt@ogilvy.com
**Personnel contact:** Same

## BBDO CHICAGO

410 N. Michigan Ave.
Chicago, IL 60611
312-337-7860
312-337-6871 (fax)
www.bbdo.com

**Employees:** 185
**Annual billings:** NA
**Number of entry level positions:** 25
**Job types:** Assistant account executive, assistant media planner, broadcast assistant, broadcast traffic coordinator, research assistant, audiovisual coordinator
**Average starting salary:** NA
**Overtime:** No
**Internship contact:** Julieann Vukovich
**Personnel contact:** Same

## BENDER, BROWNING, DOLBY & SANDERSON

444 N. Michigan Ave., Ste. 1400
Chicago, IL 60611
312-644-9600
312-644-9546 (fax)
www.bbds.com

**Employees:** 100
**Annual billings:** $39,615,000
**Number of entry-level positions:** 0
**Training program:** None
**Internships:** None
**Personnel contact:** Carol Cruz

## BURRELL COMMUNICATIONS GROUP INC.

20 N. Michigan Ave.
Chicago, IL 60602
312-443-8600
312-443-0974 (fax)

**Employees:** 100
**Annual billings:** $127,931,800
**Number of entry-level positions:** 3
**Job types:** Assistant media planner
**Average starting salary:** NA
**Overtime:** Yes
**Training program:** No
**Internships:** 10-week paid summer program in any department that requests interns
**Number of interns:** 10
**Internship contact:** Denise Williams-Harvey
**Personnel contact:** Same

## CRAMER-KRASSELT/DIRECT

225 N. Michigan Ave.
Chicago, IL 60601
312-616-9600
312-938-3157 (fax)
www.c-k.com

**Employees:** 180
**Annual billings:** $209,900,000
**Number of entry-level positions:** 20
**Job types:** assistant account executives, assistant media planners, entry-level creatives, administrative assistants
**Average starting salary:** NA
**Overtime:** Yes, for administrative assistants
**Training program:** No
**Internships:** Summer program in all departments, opportunities throughout the year depending on departmental needs; paid
**Number of interns:** 4–5 in summer
**Internship contact:** Contact appropriate department head
**Personnel contact:** Contact appropriate department head

## DDB NEEDHAM CHICAGO

200 E. Randolph Dr. 60611
312-552-6000
312-552-2396 (fax)

**Employees:** 650
**Annual billings:** $8,100,000,000
**Number of entry-level positions:** 50+
**Job types:** Account management, creative, new business, audiovisual services, finance, planning and research, interactive, digital creative, PR
**Average starting salary:** NA
**Overtime:** Depends on position

**Training program:** No
**Internships:** Participates in minority internship program run by the American Association of Advertising Agencies (4As)
**Internship contact:** Contact your local 4As office
**Personnel contact:** Jillian Bradley

## LOIS/EJL ADVERTISING

2300 Merchandise Mart
Chicago, IL 60654
312-565-3982
312-729-6401 (fax)

**Employees:** 100
**Annual billings:** $160,835,443
**Number of entry-level positions:** NA
**Job types:** Creative, account services
**Average starting salary:** NA
**Internships:** Generally in creative department, mostly through references; part-time, very flexible; some account services interns in summer; usually not paid, but some offer minimum wage
**Internship contact:** Karen Zivacki
**Personnel contact:** Same

## FOOTE, CONE & BELDING

101 E. Erie St.
Chicago, IL 60611-2897
312-751-7000
312-751-3501 (fax)

**Employees:** 650
**Annual billings:** NA
**Number of entry-level positions:** 30
**Job types:** Account management, planning, creative, media
**Average starting salary:** Depends on position
**Training program:** Account management and media, offered twice a year
**Internships:** Summer; paid
**Number of interns:** 12
**Internship contact:** Claudia Montgomery; montgomc@fcb.com
**Personnel contact:** Same

## FRANKEL & COMPANY

111 E. Wacker Dr.
Chicago, IL 60601
312-938-1900
312-938-1901(fax)
www.frankel.com

**Employees:** 700
**Annual billings:** $320,000,000
**Number of entry-level positions:** 25
**Job types:** Traffic, account coordinators, copywriters, administrative assistant
**Average starting salary:** $22,000
**Overtime:** No
**Training program:** Three-day orientation for every permanent employee
**Internships:** Summer; in account services, creative, events marketing, sports marketing, digital information services, accounting; paid
**Number of interns:** 24
**Internship contact:** Sarah Davis; sdavis@frankel.com
**Personnel contact:** Ms. Chris Shoemaker

## HAL RINEY & PARTNERS HEARTLAND

224 S. Michigan Ave, Ste. 700
Chicago, IL 60604
312-697-5700
312-697-5770 (fax)
www.riney.com

**Employees:** 85
**Annual billings:** $475,000,000
**Job types:** Administrative assistants
**Average starting salary:** $25,000
**Overtime:** Yes
**Training program:** No
**Internships:** Paid summer interns rotate between departments
**Number of interns:** 1
**Internship contact:** Lisa Shelnitz
lshelnitz@riney.com
**Personnel contact:** Brenda Mulhern

## J. WALTER THOMPSON

900 N. Michigan Ave.
Chicago, IL 60611
312-951-4000

**Employees:** 300
**Annual billings:** $873,000,000
**Number of entry-level positions:** NA
**Job types:** Account coordinator, assistant account executive, assistant media planners, junior copywriter, junior art director, broadcast/print/traffic production, finance, accounting
**Training program:** Ongoing training in account management
**Internships:** In all departments during summer; paid
**Number of interns:** 15
**Internship contact:** Jim Hutchinson
**Personnel contact:** Same

## JACK LEVY & ASSOCIATES

One S. Erie
Chicago, IL 60611
312-337-7800
312-337-1677 (fax)

**Employees:** 80
**Annual billings:** $102,000,000
**Number of entry-level positions:** 5–10
**Job types:** Mostly in traffic; no entry level positions in account management
**Average starting salary:** NA
**Internships:** Yes
**Internship contact:** Gail Gerson
**Personnel contact:** Same

## JORDAN TAMRAZ CARUSO ADVERTISING

1419 N. Wells St.
Chicago, IL 60610-1395
312-951-2000
312-951-8475 (fax)

**Employees:** 115
**Annual billings:** $71,400,000
**Number of entry-level positions:** 15
**Job types:** All departments
**Average starting salary:** $18,000–$25,000
**Overtime:** No
**Training program:** No
**Internships:** Year-round in account management, once in a while in creative; both paid and unpaid
**Number of interns:** 2–3
**Internships contact:** Liz Boon
**Personnel contact:** Arlin Hale

## THE LEAP PARTNERSHIP

22 W. Hubbard St.
Chicago, IL 60610
312-494-0300
312-494-0120 (fax)
www.leapnet.com

**Employees:** 60
**Annual billings:** $250,000,000
**Number of entry-level positions:** 6
**Job types:** Creative
**Average starting salary:** $24,000–$28,000
**Overtime:** No
**Training program:** No
**Internships:** No; possibly developing program in the future
**Personnel contact:** Christine Varrett; varrett@leapnet.com

## LEO BURNETT COMPANY

35 W. Wacker Dr.
Chicago, IL 60601
312-220-5959
312-220-3299 (fax)
www.leoburnett.com

**Employees:** 2,000
**Annual billings:** $7,927,600,000
**Number of entry-level positions:** 200 "professional," approximately 100 "paraprofessional"
**Job types:** Client services associates, copywriters, art directors, media trainees
**Average starting salary:** $25,000–$30,000 for recent college grad
**Overtime:** Depending on position
**Training program:** Client services, media, creative
**Internships:** During the summer, paid, mostly for minority students; opportunities in client services, creative, media
**Internship contact:** Jackie Skowronek; hyperlink Jackie_Skowronek@Chi.LeoBurnett.com
**Personnel contact:** Same
**Recruitment:** Northwestern, University of Illinois, University of Michigan, The Portfolio Center, University of Texas

## MCCONNAUGHY STEIN SCHMIDT BROWN

North Pier, 401 E. Illinois St., Ste. 500
Chicago, IL 60611
312-321-8000
312-321-8008 (fax)

**Employees:** 55
**Annual billings:** $84,752,320
**Number of entry-level positions:** 3
**Job types:** Account assistant
**Average starting salary:** $20,000–$24,000
**Overtime:** Yes
**Training program:** No
**Internships:** Summer and sometimes during the year in account services, creative, media, research/planning; unpaid
**Number of interns:** 5
**Internship contact:** Mary Gremmler
**Personnel contact:** Same

## KETCHUM DIRECTORY ADVERTISING/CHICAGO

205 N. Michigan Ave., Ste. 3400
Chicago, IL 60601
312-228-6800
312-228-6900 (fax)
www.ketchum.com

**Employees:** 50
**Annual billings:** $1,062,000,000
**Number of entry-level positions:** 25–30
**Job types:** Mostly account service representatives, operations coordinator, support staff
**Average starting salary:** $20,000
**Overtime:** Yes
**Training program:** In the process of developing a training program called "Ketchum College"
**Internships:** In account services department; 1 intern per quarter; both paid and unpaid
**Number of interns:** 4
**Internship contact:** Susan.harris@ketchum.com
**Personnel contact:** Same

## N.W. AYER & PARTNERS CHICAGO

515 N. State St., Ste. 2100
Chicago, IL 60610
312-644-2937
312-644-4123 (fax)

**Employees:** 20
**Annual billings:** $851,900,000 (worldwide)
**Number of entry-level positions:** 0
**Training program:** No
**Internships:** No
**Personnel contact:** Kim Nimtz

## OGILVY & MATHER

One Illinois Ctr. Bldg, 111 E. Wacker
Chicago, IL 60601-4208
312-856-8200
312-856-8207 (fax)

**Annual billings:** $7,600,000,000
**Number of entry-level positions:** NA
**Job types:** Most are in media
**Average starting salary:** NA
**Training program:** No
**Internships:** Mainly in the summer, depending on need; a few during the year
**Internship contact:** Patti Grace
**Personnel contact:** Same

## RAPP COLLINS/CHICAGO

Ten S. Riverside Plaza, Ste. 1920
Chicago, IL 60606
312-454-0660
312-454-0442 (fax)

**Employees:** 80
**Annual billings:** $594,794,000
**Number of entry-level positions:** 6
**Job types:** Account coordinators
**Average starting salary:** $18,500–23,000
**Overtime:** Where appropriate by law
**Training program:** No, in the process of addressing issue
**Internships:** No, in the process of addressing issue
**Personnel contact:** Vera McRae

## YOUNG & RUBICAM CHICAGO

One S. Wacker Dr., Ste. 1800
Chicago, IL 60606
312-845-4000
312-845-2800 (fax)
www.yr.com

**Employees:** 88
**Annual billings:** $9,900,000,000 (worldwide)

**Number of entry-level positions:** 10
**Job types:** Advertising assistants
**Average starting salary:** NA
**Overtime:** Yes
**Training program:** Internal training in all departments except creative
**Internships:** Summer; in any department that has the need; paid
**Number of interns:** 1
**Internship contact:** Ms. Kelly Langford
kelly_langford@yr.com
**Personnel contact:** Same

# ASSOCIATIONS — CHICAGO

## AMERICAN MARKETING ASSOCIATION (AMA)

250 S. Wacker Sr., Ste. 200
Chicago, IL 60606
312-648-0536
www.ama.org

The AMA, comprised of marketing practitioners, educators, and students, is the world's largest association of marketing professionals. There are currently 390 AMA collegiate chapters providing 16,000 student members with knowledge, skills, and practical experience that cannot be gained in the classroom alone. By participating in activities and joining committees, you can gain practical marketing, advertising, management, and promotion skills that will increase your value and make you more competitive in the advertising industry.

AMA student members can take advantage of the following:

*International Collegiate Conference:* Provides students with career information and leadership training.

*Marketing Challenge Competition:* Allows participating chapters to gain hands-on experience developing a professional marketing plan.

*Annual Awards Program:* Recognizes collegiate chapters excelling in professional marketing services.

*Marketing News:* AMA student members receive nine issues of the newsletter each year, which contain articles on the marketing profession, its players, trends, and news analysis.

## THE ACCOUNT PLANNING GROUP

c/o McConnaughy Stein Schmidt Brown
North Pier, 401 E. Illinois St., Ste. 500
Chicago, IL 60611
312-321-8075
www.mssb.com/apgchicago
Contact: David Rabjohns

The account planning group is a place for planners to get together and meet. Planners from around the world speak at monthly events, which are free to anyone interested in the field. Lunch or evening meetings are generally held the second Monday of each month at various agencies. "We have a 30-minute presentation, then sit around and debate the topic. Our atmosphere is very low-key and friendly, and people who are out of a job come to network." Our goal is to ultimately provide training and education," says David. "Planning is an exploding field and everybody is looking to hire planners. Fallon has entry-level jobs, so does TBWA/Chiat Day, and Kirshenbaum and Bond has ten or twenty. Los Angeles is at the forefront of the planning industry, followed by New York. Chicago is just getting into the wave but it is the fastest growing city for planners."

## CHICAGO ADVERTISING FEDERATION

4700 W. Lake Ave.
Glenview, IL 60025
847-375-4728

Holds monthly events, career days, luncheons with guest speakers, and mentoring program; publishes *The Voice* newsletter. Individual membership is $100.00/year, student rate is $35.00/year.

## CHICAGO PORTFOLIO REVIEW

116 W. Illinois St.
Chicago, IL 60610
312-321-9405
www.chicagoportfolio.com
Contact: Jeff Epstein

Holds copywriting and art direction classes taught by agency experts. Evening classes are held once a week for eight weeks, with four sessions per year; fee is $375.00 per class. Also hosts the Chicago Show, a local advertising award show that includes a student competition.

## MCCONNAUGHY STEIN SCHMIDT BROWN

North Pier, 401 E. Illinois St., Ste. 500
Chicago, IL 60611
312-321-8000
Contact: Kevin Lynch

This agency's creative department hosts a monthly student portfolio review. Hopeful creatives can meet with the agency's staff of ten and get a critique of their work. Meetings are held on the second Thursday of every month about nine months out of the year; they are free, informal, and no specific skill level is required.

## WOMEN'S ADVERTISING CLUB

30 N. Michigan Ave., Ste. 508
Chicago, IL 60602
312-263-2215

Holds monthly meetings for the group's 190 members; offers networking and a job bank; $60 annual fee.

# RECRUITERS — CHICAGO

## AD PROS/AD TEMPS

311 W. Superior St., Ste. 500
Chicago, IL 60610
312-751-0090
630-571-9900 (Oakbrook office)
adprofessionals.com
adtemps.com
Contact: Chris Murray

Ad Pros works with Chicago and other midwestern advertising agencies, as well as marketing and promotions companies to place recent college grads in all types of positions, such as assistant account executives and assistant media planners and buyers (including media training programs at large agencies), as well as art and copy positions. If you want to pursue a creative position, it is to your advantage to be proficient with QuarkXpress, Illustrator, and Photoshop, advises Chris.

"Agencies look for people who are self-starters, motivated, and take initiative. They want people who are focused and have a proven passion for the industry," observes Chris. If you get your foot in the door with a clerical position, make sure you ask the right questions, she cautions. "Find out whether the position is promotable. In a larger agency you may not be able to forge a career out of an administrative job, but with a small or mid-size company, it may lead to an executive position."

Ad Pros also holds an annual job fair for people interested in entry-level advertising. Chicago ad agencies have picked up lots of new business lately, says Chris, and the market is growing.

## THE JOB NETWORK

P.O. Box 267934
Chicago, IL 60626
773-274-1093
Contact: Kathy Short

Offers a monthly job bulletin with employment listings from top professional communication companies including advertising, marketing, and public relations. Members of the Women's Advertising Club receive the publication free of charge; for others the cost is $20.00 for three months, $60.00 per year. First issue is complimentary.

## LEE WEIL & ASSOCIATES

205 W. Wacker Dr., Ste. 901
Chicago, IL 60606
312-578-0828

Places candidates in marketing, market research, and planning positions.

## PATRICIA STEVENS

27 E. Monroe, Ste. 600
Chicago, IL 60603
312-726-3030

## THE AMY BURACK COMPANY

444 N. Michigan
Chicago, IL 60611
312-527-2505
www.amyburack.com
Contact: Amy Burack

"Internships are key in getting your first job," says Amy Burack, who works with candidates with at least one year of experience and places people in advertising, promotion, and direct marketing in all major cities. Clients include BBDO, Bozell, Leo Burnett, DMB&B, Draft Worldwide, Frankel and Company, McConnaughy Stein Schmidt Brown, and more. But don't rely on recruiters to find you a job, she says. Employers don't want to pay for a recruiter to find them someone who has no experience. Use your contacts and your alumni, she recommends.

"Finding a job is a lot about attitude. You should know what you want but you should also be flexible. I look for people who are mature, thoughtful, passionate, and distinguish themselves with their ambition. Clear written and verbal skills are also essential. I read a resume from the bottom up. What are your interests? I look at the person as an overall package."

## SANDY WADE

330 N. Wabash, Ste. 2901
Chicago, IL 60611
312-595-3200
sandy@swco.com

# AGENCIES — DALLAS/HOUSTON

## BATES/SOUTHWEST

5847 San Felipe, Ste. 400
Houston, TX 77057
713-266-7676
713-267-7222 (fax)

**Employees:** 80
**Annual billings:** $5,111,521,000 (worldwide)
**Number of entry-level positions:** 3
**Job types:** Account service
**Average starting salary:** $20,000–$25,000
**Overtime:** Yes
**Training program:** No
**Internships:** In all departments only during summer; paid for undergrads
**Number of interns:** 10
**Internship contact:** Sue Wiseman
**Personnel contact:** Same

## BERRY-BROWN ADVERTISING

3100 McKinnon, Ste. 1100
Dallas, TX 75201-1046
214-871-1001
214-871-1137 (fax)

**Employees:** 62
**Annual billings:** $51,400,000
**Number of entry-level positions:** 10
**Job types:** Creative, media, account services
**Average starting salary:** $20,000–$27,000
**Overtime:** Yes
**Training program:** Yes
**Internships:** Year-round in creative, account service, media; paid and for credit
**Number of interns:** 4
**Internship contact:** Virdie Horton
**Personnel contact:** Same

## DDB NEEDHAM DALLAS/TLP PARTNERSHIP

200 Crescent Ct.
Dallas, TX 75201
214-599-5500
or 855-2252

See TLP listing

## EVANSGROUP

3100 Monticello Ave.
Dallas, TX 75205
214-520-1200
214-520-0364 (fax)

**Employees:** 60
**Annual billings:** $290,000,000
**Number of entry-level positions:** 6
**Job types:** All departments including creative
**Average starting salary:** $21,000–$24,000
**Overtime:** Yes
**Training program:** No
**Internships:** Year-round in all departments; paid
**Number of interns:** 4–5
**Internship contact:** Tom Bolger; tbolger@evansgroup.com
**Personnel contact:** Same

## FOGARTY KLEIN & PARTNERS

7155 Old Katy Rd., Ste. 100
Houston, TX 77024
713-862-5100
713-869-6560 (fax)

**Employees:** 135
**Annual billings:** $140,000,000
**Number of entry-level positions:** 10
**Job types:** Account coordinator, junior media buyer/planner, junior art director, creative assistant, account services, public relations
**Average starting salary:** NA
**Overtime:** No
**Training program:** No
**Internships:** Year-round in all departments for college credit only
**Number of interns:** NA
**Internship contact:** Debbi Ray
**Personnel contact:** Same

## HADELER SULLIVAN EWING

Three Lincoln Centre
5430 LBJ Frwy., Ste. 1100
Dallas, TX 75240
972-776-8000
972-776-8080 (fax)
www.hslgroup.com

**Employees:** 45
**Annual billings:** $45,000,000
**Number of entry-level positions:** 5
**Job types:** Assistant account executive
**Average starting salary:** $20,000, depending on experience
**Overtime:** No
**Training program:** Revamping
**Internships:** 3 times/year, year-round and summer in account service and creative; paid
**Number of interns:** 9–10
**Internship contact:** Brenda Myers; brenda_myers@hslgroup.com
**Personnel contact:** Same

## JWT SPECIALIZED COMMUNICATIONS

350 N. St. Paul, Ste. 1500
Dallas, TX 75201
214-855-5155
214-871-7204 (fax)

**Employees:** 40
**Annual billings:** $2,000,000,000 (worldwide)
**Number of entry-level positions:** 5
**Job types:** Account coordinator, production/traffic coordinator, junior creative
**Average starting salary:** $20,000–$25,000
**Overtime:** Yes, for coordinator positions; depends on title
**Training program:** No
**Internships:** Paid, year-round in all departments
**Number of interns:** 3 in spring/summer, 1 in winter
**Internship contact:** Lynne Treachler; lynne.treachler@jwtworks.com
**Personnel contact:** Same

## KWGC

2 Turtle Creek Tower
3838 Oak Lawn Ave., Ste. 1300
Dallas, TX 75219
214-987-4377
214-528-2862 (fax)
www.kwgc.com

**Employees:** 20
**Annual billings:** $20,500,000
**Number of entry-level positions:** 1
**Job types:** Account service
**Average starting salary:** $18,000–$24,000
**Overtime:** No

**Training program:** No
**Internships:** One at a time during each semester in creative or account service; unpaid
**Number of interns:** About 4
**Internship contact:** Creative: John Kraus; john@kwgc.com
**Account service:** Ruby Dimarob; ruby@kwgc.com
**Personnel contact:** Same

## LARKIN MEEDER & SCHWEIDEL

2501 Cedar Springs Rd., Ste. 400
Dallas, TX 75201
214-979-5000
214-979-5005 (fax)

**Employees:** 65
**Annual billings:** $102,000,000
**Number of entry-level positions:** 4
**Job types:** Media, clerical, creative/Macintosh artists
**Average starting salary:** $18,000–$23,000
**Overtime:** Yes
**Training program:** No
**Internships:** Sporadically throughout the year in any department; paid
**Number of interns:** 2–3
**Internship contact:** Penny Pleuckhahn
**Personnel contact:** Same

## MCCANN ERICKSON

Houston, TX
713-965-0303
713-439-9349 (fax)

**Employees:** 100
**Annual billings:** $7,178,000,000 (worldwide)
**Number of entry-level positions:** 5
**Job types:** Media, research, account service
**Average starting salary:** $21,000–$26,000
**Overtime:** Yes
**Training program:** No
**Internships:** In all departments including media, creative, account service, production; paid
**Number of interns:** 4
**Internship contact:** Delores Brownlow; deloresbrownlow@mccann.com
**Personnel contact:** Same

## MOROCH & ASSOC., INC.

3625 N. Hall, Ste. 1200
Dallas, TX 75219
214-520-9700
214-520-6464 (fax)
www.moroch.com

**Employees:** 80
**Annual billings:** $37,000,000
**Number of entry-level positions:** 20
**Job types:** Majority in account services, media
**Average starting salary:** $18,000–$21,000
**Overtime:** Yes
**Training program:** Internal
**Internships:** Year-round in all departments; unpaid
**Number of interns:** 8 during summer; 2–3 during year
**Internship contact:** Teresa McCormack; tmccormack@moroch.com
**Personnel contact:** Kathy Beath

## PUBLICIS/BLOOM

3500 Maple Ave., Ste. 450
Dallas, TX 75219
214-443-9900
214-443-0701 (fax)
www.p/b.com

**Employees:** 242
**Annual billings:** $319,900,000
**Number of entry-level positions:** 20–25
**Job types:** Assistant account executive, assistant media planner, production assistant, junior positions in copy/art
**Average starting salary:** Assistant account executive/planner: $20,000–$22,000; copywriter: $25,000; broadcast: $20,000+
**Overtime:** No
**Training program:** No
**Internships:** For college credit year-round (prefer to have interns during year); in account service, media planning; thinking of starting scholarship program paying $300–$500 toward interns' tuition
**Number of interns:** 6 during summer
**Internship contact:** Pat Fabby; pat_fabby@p/b.com
**Personnel contact:** Debi Lockhart

## TAYLOR-SMITH GROUP

2000 W. Loop S., 16th Fl.
Houston, TX 77027
713-877-1220
713-877-1672 (fax)

**Employees:** 38
**Annual billings:** NA
**Number of entry-level positions:** 6–10
**Job types:** Media coordinator, administrative assistant
**Average starting salary:** NA
**Overtime:** No
**Training program:** Internal
**Internships:** During summer in traffic and media; paid
**Number of interns:** 2
**Internship contact:** Susan Hagler; beanorange@aol.com
**Personnel contact:** Same

## TLP

200 Crescent Ct., Ste. 800
Dallas, TX 75201
214-871-5600
214-855-2199 (fax)

**Employees:** 500
**Annual billings:** $300,000,000
**Number of entry-level positions:** NA
**Job types:** All departments
**Average starting salary:** NA
**Training program:** Account management
**Internships:** All departments during summer
**Number of interns:** 30
**Internship contact:** Sandy Notly
**Personnel contact:** Tammy Morris

## TMP WORLDWIDE

12225 Greenville Ave., Ste. 750
Dallas, TX 75243
972-479-9193
972-479-0320 (fax)
www.tmp.com

**Employees:** 55
**Annual billings:** $1,012,000,000
**Entry-level Positions:** 5

**Job types:** Account coordinator, account rep., research coordinator

**Average starting salary:** $21,000–$26,500

**Overtime:** Yes

**Training program:** No

**Internships:** Year-round in recruitment and yellow-pages divisions; mostly paid, some unpaid

**Number of interns:** 3

**Internship contact:** Sandra Clerk

Personnel contact: Julie Sliva; jsliva@tmp.com

# ASSOCIATIONS — DALLAS/HOUSTON

## DALLAS ADVERTISING LEAGUE

P.O. Box 800863
Dallas, TX 75380
214-363-9872
Ad2 InfoLine - 972-994-3567
www.uta.edu/student_orgs/ad3/ad2dall.htm

The Dallas Ad league focuses on preparing young professionals to become more knowledgeable, productive, and marketable in their careers by helping them to keep their skills and talents fresh, gain experience, and build a network of peers. The group offers courses in all advertising disciplines and holds monthly events and seminars.

## HOUSTON ADVERTISING FEDERATION

P.O. Box 27592
Houston, TX 77227
(713) ADS-9999
rampages.onramp.net/~billbits/haf.html

HAF sponsors a job bank that is available online to both members and nonmembers and lists full-time positions as well as internships. The group also publishes the *HAFtime* newsletter, also available online. Associate membership for people under the age of 30 is $100.00 with a one-time initiation fee of $25.00.

# RECRUITERS — DALLAS/HOUSTON

## ART SQUAD

5550 LBJ Freeway, Ste. 215
Dallas, TX 75240
972-419-1767
www.artsquad.com
Contact: Connie Dye

Art Squad places art directors and copywriters in Dallas and Houston. Potential creatives meet recruiters face to face for a three-hour screening process, which includes a portfolio review and software testing. Also places production/traffic managers who should have more than one year of experience or a strong internship. "There is a lot of competition to work in an agency environment. But there are lots of positions, particularly in graphic design, which is growing very quickly in the Dallas area."

## ADVANTAGE STAFFING SERVICES

12770 Merit Dr., Ste. 115
Dallas, TX 75251
972-774-0600
Contact: Dean Crawford

Handles design, desktop, and graphics positions.

## MARKET SEARCH

PO Box 800876
Dallas, TX 75380
972-418-7141

Private recruiting company run by the head of human resources at Larkin Meeder & Schweidel.

## SEARCH COM

12900 Preston Rd.
Dallas, TX 75230
214-490-0300

Exeutive search firm specializing in advertising, marketing, and public relations; but places employees into jobs with minimum salaries of $20,000.

# AGENCIES — LOS ANGELES

## ASHER & PARTNERS

5900 Wilshire Blvd.
Los Angeles, CA 90036
213-931-4151
213-931-4548 (fax)

**Employees:** 75
**Annual billings:** $105,000,000
**Number of entry-level positions:** 8
**Job types:** Executive assistant, account coordinator, media assistant
**Average starting salary:** $25,000
**Overtime:** For some positions
**Training program:** Internal
**Internships:** Year-round in all departments on an as-needed basis
**Internship contact:** Pat Pellicano
**Personnel contact:** Same

## BBDO WEST

10960 Wilshire Blvd., 16th Fl.
Los Angeles, CA 90024
310-444-4500
310-444-4555 (fax)

**Employees:** 150
**Annual billings:** $5,634,000,000 (worldwide)
**Number of entry-level positions:** 20
**Job types:** Account services, media planning, and media buying
**Average starting salary:** $21,000
**Overtime:** Yes
**Training program:** No formal training; entry-level employees learn basics from upper management in a mentor program
**Internships:** Year-round in account services, media buying and planning, none in creative; unpaid
**Number of interns:** 5–10
**Internship contact:** Carolyn Mathis; cmathis@bbdowest.com
**Personnel contact:** Jean Ann Hutchinson

## DDB NEEDHAM LOS ANGELES

11601 Wilshire Blvd.
Los Angeles, CA 90025
310-996-5700
310-996-5890 (fax)
www.ddbn.com

**Employees:** 160 (220 w/freelancers)
**Annual billings:** $8,100,000,000
**Number of entry-level positions:** 25 (office has high turnover)
**Job types:** Account coordinator, media assistant (planning and buying), account assistant, creative assistant, print production assistant, traffic assistant, human resources assistant
**Average starting salary:** $18,000–$23,000
**Overtime:** Yes
**Training program:** No
**Internships:** Paid, in all departments on an as-needed basis
**Number of interns:** 12
**Internship contact:** cwilliams@la.ddbn.com
**Personnel contact:** Same

## DAILEY AND ASSOCIATES

3055 Wilshire Blvd.
Los Angeles, CA 90010
213-386-7823
213-380-6655 (fax)
www.daileyads.com

**Employees:** 200
**Annual billings:** $27,000,000
**Number of entry-level positions:** several
**Job types:** Reception, mailroom, account assistant (promotable after 1 year), traffic, production, creative
**Average starting salary:** $22,000
**Overtime:** Yes
**Training program:** No
**Internships:** Traffic, account management, depending on need; paid; runs minority intern program
**Internship contact:** John Crosson
**Personnel contact:** Toby Burke

## DEUTSCH

**Employees:** 50 and growing
**Annual billings:** $330,000,000
**Number of entry-level positions:** 5

**Job types:** Account coordinator, media assistant, administrative, receptionist
**Average starting salary:** Low $20,000s
**Overtime:** For administrative only
**Training program:** Establishing loosely structured on-the-job program for next year that includes seminars
**Internships:** In all departments on an as-needed basis; none in LA office; evaluating pay structure
**Internship contact:** Kristin Greeves
**Personnel contact:** Same

## EJL ADVERTISING/LOS ANGELES

5700 Wilshire Blvd.
Los Angeles, CA 90036
213-932-1234
213-932-6134 (fax)

**Employees:** 41
**Annual billings:** $160,835,443
**Number of entry-level positions:** 2
**Job types:** Account coordinator, clerical
**Average starting salary:** $16,000–$20,000
**Overtime:** No
**Training program:** No
**Internships:** Paid and unpaid in media and account service during summer
**Number of interns:** 1
**Internship contact:** Dennis Coe; dcoe@ejl.com
**Personnel contact:** Same

## EVANSGROUP

5757 Wilshire Blvd.
Los Angeles, CA 90036
213-954-3000
213-931-1257 (fax)
www.evansgroup.com

**Employees:** 70
**Annual billings:** $290,000,000
**Number of entry-level positions:** NA
**Job types:** Account coordinator, media assistant, associate art director, publicity assistant (in entertainment division)
**Average starting salary:** NA
**Overtime:** No
**Training program:** No
**Internships:** Year-round in account services, media, production, public relations (entertainment division); paid and unpaid

**Number of interns:** 5–6 during summer
**Internship contact:** Advertising: Sonya Shemdin; Entertainment: Sasha Lord
**Personnel contact:** David Meaghan

## FOOTE, CONE & BELDING

11601 Wilshire Blvd.
Los Angeles, CA 90025
310-312-7000
310-479-1277 (fax)

**Employees:** 80
**Annual billings:** $155,000,000
**Number of entry-level positions:** 9
**Job types:** Account management, traffic
**Average starting salary:** $22,000
**Overtime:** Yes
**Training program:** No
**Internships:** Year-round for course credit only in account service, broadcast production, research, media
**Number of interns:** 7
**Internship contact:** Rosanna Ortiz
**Personnel contact:** Mary Piatti

## GREY ADVERTISING, WESTERN DIVISION

6100 Wilshire Blvd.
Los Angeles, CA 90048
213-936-6060
213-937-5798 (fax)

**Employees:** 168
**Annual billings:** $593,317,000 (worldwide)
**Number of entry-level positions:** 40
**Job types:** Account management, media
**Average starting salary:** $20,000–$25,000
**Overtime:** Yes
**Training program:** The "account management development program," an ongoing, intensive, two-year training program
**Internships:** Agency works with students to match interests; summer and sometimes fall program, unpaid if student receives course credit
**Number of interns:** 3
**Internship contact:** Stu Hardman
**Personnel contact:** Joy Walden; joy_walden@greywest.com

## IMADA WONG COMMUNICATIONS GROUP

633 W. Fifth St., Ste. 2020
Los Angeles, CA 90071
213-627-4476
imadawong@worldnet.att.net

**Employees:** 18 full-time, 4 part-time
**Annual billings:** $2,800,000
**Number of entry-level positions:** 0
**Internships:** Depends on work and new accounts; generally in all departments, paid
**Number of interns:** 6
**Internship contact:** Contact individual group heads

## JWT SPECIALIZED COMMUNICATIONS

6500 Wilshire Blvd., 21st Fl.
Los Angeles, CA 90048
213-951-1500
213-655-9285(fax)
www.jwtworks.com

**Employees:** 130+
**Annual billings:** $2,000,000,000 (worldwide)
**Number of entry-level positions:** 20
**Job types:** Account services, research; agency looks for people with a few years of experience; job listings posted at local colleges and in the *LA Times*
**Average starting salary:** NA
**Internships:** Agency participates in the American Association of Advertising Agencies' multicultural internship program; paid
**Internship contact:** Contact your local 4A's office
**Personnel contact:** Julie Rowee

## LA AGENCIA DE ORCI & ASOCIADOS

11620 Wilshire Blvd., 6th Fl.
Los Angeles, CA 90025
310-444-7300
310-478-3587 (fax)
www.laagencia.com

**Employees:** 45
**Annual billings:** NA
**Number of entry-level positions:** Many, due to reorganization
**Job types:** Account clerks, administrative
**Average starting salary:** NA
**Training program:** Seminars and classes at UCLA

**Internships:** Year-round, in all departments, for grade or pay
**Number of interns:** NA
**Internship contact:** Sergio Muñoz; smunoz@laagencia.com
**Personnel contact:** Same

## MUSE CORDERO CHEN

6100 Wilshire Blvd., Ste. 1600
Los Angeles, CA 90048
213-954-1655
213-954-9171 (fax)
www.musecordero.com

**Employees:** 30
**Annual billings:** $27,000,000
**Number of entry-level positions:** 1
**Job types:** Receptionist
**Average starting salary:** $18,000–$22,000
**Overtime:** Yes
**Training program:** No
**Internships:** Participates in the 4A's minority program for college students, an 8-week paid summer internship
**Number of interns:** 1
**Internship contact:** Wanda Jackson at the American Association of Advertising Agencies
**Personnel contact:** Rob Schlief; rob@musecordero.com

## PANCOM INTERNATIONAL

3701 Wilshire Blvd., #800
Los Angeles, CA 90010
213-383-6729
www.pancom.com

**Employees:** 27
**Annual billings:** $27,000,000
**Number of entry-level positions:** 2–3
**Job types:** Account executive
**Average starting salary:** $30,000–$35,000
**Overtime:** No
**Training program:** Sends employees to 4A's seminars
**Internships:** Account services; year-round, paid
**Internship contact:** Joseph Choi; jospeh@pancom.com
**Personnel contact:** Same

## THE PHELPS GROUP

11999 San Vincente Blvd., 4th Fl.
Los Angeles, CA 90049
310-471-6170
310-471-2830 (fax)
www.phelpsgroup.com

**Employees:** 50
**Annual billings:** $22,000,000
**Number of entry-level positions:** 8
**Job types:** Account coordinator, media assistant
**Average starting salary:** $18,000–$30,000
**Overtime:** No
**Training program:** Internal in all departments
**Internships:** Interns are recent grads or working on Master's; positions are year-round and flexible; paid.
**Number of interns:** 6 full-time, 15 throughout year
**Internship contact:** Glenn Schieke; glenn@phelpsgroup.com
**Personnel contact:** Same

## POPPE TYSON

12121 Wilshire Blvd.
Los Angeles, CA 90025
310-447-3300
310-447-7081 (fax)
www.poppe.com

**Employees:** 50
**Annual billings:** $110,000,000
**Number of entry-level positions:** NA
**Job types:** Traffic assistant, production assistant, account coordinator, group assistant (no creative positions)
**Average starting salary:** NA
**Overtime:** Yes, depending on position
**Training program:** Implementing basic entry-level program
**Internships:** Summer; paid
**Number of interns:** 1
**Internship contact:** Elizabeth Gaudio; egaudio@la.poppe.com
**Personnel contact:** Same

## SUISSA MILLER ADVERTISING

11601 Wilshire Blvd., 16th Fl.
Los Angeles, CA 90025
310-392-9666
310-392-2625 (fax)
www.suissamiller.com

**Employees:** 150
**Annual billings:** $119,000,000
**Number of entry-level positions:** NA
**Job types:** All departments
**Average starting salary:** NA
**Training program:** No
**Internships:** In creative and account services during the summer; paid and unpaid
**Number of interns:** 4
**Internship contact:** Varies from year to year
**Personnel contact:** Jenny Lebetsamer

## WESTERN INTERNATIONAL MEDIA CORPORATION

8544 Sunset Blvd.
Los Angeles, CA 90069
310-659-5711
310-652-1373 (fax)

**Employees:** 1,700+ nationwide
**Annual billings:** $2,395,000,000
**Number of entry-level positions:** 300–400 nationwide
**Job types:** Assistant account executive, account coordinator, assistant media planner, broadcast assistant, research assistant, assistant network/print buyer
**Average starting salary:** NA
**Overtime:** NA
**Training program:** NA
**Internships:** Account services, media, planning, and research from June through September; paid
**Number of interns:** 15–20
**Internship contact:** Human resources
**Personnel contact:** Meredith Hauger

## VALDES ZACKY ASSOCIATES

1875 Century Park E., Ste. 1000
Los Angeles, CA 90067
310-557-0811
310-286-1903 (fax)
www.valdeszacky.com

**Employees:** 30
**Annual billings:** $15,000,000
**Number of entry-level positions:** 2
**Job types:** Client service, administrative
**Average starting salary:** $22,000–$28,000
**Overtime:** No
**Training program:** No
**Internships:** Sometimes in account service and creative; unpaid
**Number of interns:** 0 last year
**Internship contact:** Department heads
**Personnel contact:** Laura Nole

# ASSOCIATIONS — LOS ANGELES

## AMERICAN MARKETING ASSOCIATION

127-8 Street
Hermosa Beach 90254
310-966-4654
Contact: Lori Lee Murphee

See description under Chicago listing

## ADVERTISING CLUB OF LOS ANGELES

6404 Wilshire Blvd., Ste. 1111
Los Angeles, CA 90048
213-782-1044
www.wsaaa.org/index.html

Ad2 Los Angeles, a division of the Advertising Club of Los Angeles, is comprised of advertising and marketing professionals under the age of 31. The group fosters "mentor" relationships between Ad2 Members and ad industry professionals through collaborative projects and volunteer work, and provides networking opportunities for young executives. Events include educational meetings, social activities, such as the annual ski trip and "AdJam", leadership workshops, and other advertising-related activities.
Members can become involved in one of five committees (social, membership, career development, public service, and creative) and develop an advertising campaign for a local non-profit. In addition to developing the overall strategy and creative, Ad2 produces the ads, places them in media, including TV, radio, print, and outdoor, and manages public relations activities.

Ad2 membership is open to people under 31 years of age. There is no initiation fee; dues are $45.00/year.

The Advertising Club of Los Angeles also sponsors the Minority Advertising Training Program (M.A.T.), a coalition of the Western States Advertising Agencies Association, the Advertising Club of Los Angeles, and TBWA/Chiat Day. The program extends paid 13-week internships in advertising agencies, public relations firms, print, and broadcast media to minority college students and graduates. To qualify, you must be a minority college student (junior, senior, recent graduate, or Master's candidate) with a 2.7 grade point average or better in any major.

The M.A.T. Program has successfully placed nearly 300 minority interns in the advertising and broadcasting field, and more than 100 interns have been hired for full-time positions by their employers following their internship period.

## LOS ANGELES CREATIVE CLUB

6404 Wilshire Blvd., Ste. 1111
Los Angeles, CA 90048
213-655-1951

The LA Creative Club holds a student advertising competition once a year.

# RECRUITERS — LOS ANGELES

## CHRIS CARD

2049 Century Park E., Ste. 1200
Los Angeles, CA 90067
310-556-8866

The advertising business is booming on the West coast, according to Chris Card. She deals with candidates who have at least one year experience for jobs in account management and media. Clients include Los Angeles ad agencies, with affiliate offices in Chicago and New York. Agencies desperately need media planners, she says, and there are definitely more media jobs out there than account management. "You need to pound the pavement to get a job in account service, and express an overwhelming interest in the field and a willingness to start at any level to get a foot in the door. Although it's beneficial to have an ultimate focus, you need to do whatever it takes to break in and that may mean taking an administrative job. However, keep in mind that many agencies promote employees in administrative positions."

## AD PERSONNEL

315 S. Beverly Dr., Ste. 201
Beverly Hills, CA 90212
310-284-3939
Contact: John Smerling

Ad Personnel is a "boutique employment agency" that places recent college grads in account services as "group assistants" or "coordinators" as well as in media positions. John works with ten or twelve advertising agencies including Grey and Foote, Cone & Belding, as well as media houses such as Katz and Western International Media. Use a recruiter as just one angle of your job search, he recommends. Many agencies recruit at schools and search for candidates on their own before paying an outside consultant to do so, especially for an entry-level position. "Young people's expectations of what they can attain right out of school are often very different from reality. Keep in mind that the bulk of your work will be administrative when you start out, but at the same time, many agencies, like Dailey & Associates for example, want everyone from the receptionist on up to grow and they do their best to promote their employees, even temps." Southern California's economy is strong, according to John. The entertainment and media industries drive this market and although there is no lack of applicants to fill jobs, there are "tons of openings."

Finding that first job "all boils down to image, personality, and chemistry along with your ability to exhibit a sense of savvy, confidence, and a burning desire to be in this business."

# AGENCIES—NEW YORK CITY

## ADLER BOSCHETTO PEEBLES & PARTNERS

136 Madison Avenue, 12th Floor
New York, NY 10016
212-684-5220
212-684-0469 (fax)

**Employees:** 110
**Annual billings:** $120,000,000
**Number of entry-level positions:** 5–10
**Job types:** Assistant media planner, assistant account executive, junior copywriter, production coordinator, administrative assistant
**Average starting salary:** $23,000–$30,000
**Overtime:** No
**Training program:** No
**Internships:** Fall, spring, summer in media, creative, account management; paid
**Number of interns:** 8
**Internship contact:** Elizabeth Connelly
**Personnel contact:** Same

## AMMIRATI PURIS LINTAS WORLDWIDE

One Dag Hammarskjold Plaza
New York, NY 10017
212-605-8000
212-605-4709 (fax)

**Employees:** 700
**Annual billings:** $5,653,409,000
**Number of entry-level positions:** NA
**Job types:** Staff assistants in all departments. After 8–12 months you can be promoted to assistant account executive. If you've interned you may be able to start at a higher level.
**Average starting salary:** $18,000–$20,000
**Training program:** None
**Internships:** College juniors can participate in a three-month paid internship over the summer. Students usually have referrals from within the agency.
**Personnel contact:** Andrea Fessler

## ANGOTTI, THOMAS, HEDGE

119 Fifth Avenue
New York, NY 10003
212-973-2100
212-867-2656 (fax)

**Employees:** 110
**Annual billings:** $193,000,000
**Number of entry-level positions:** 4
**Job types:** Administrative assistants. Five account
  coordinator positions were filled by MBAs.
**Starting Salary:** $18,000–$22,000 (for AAs)
**Training program:** None
**Internships:** Paid and unpaid internships are
  available over the summer. Departments TBA
  each year.
**Number of interns:** 5
**Personnel contact:** Cheryl Proto

## AVRETT, FREE & GINSBERG, INC.

800 Third Avenue
New York, NY 10022
212-832-3800
212-759-9505 (fax)

**Employees:** 150
**Annual billings:** $368,000,000
**Number of entry-level positions:** 3
**Job types:** Assistant account executives
**Average starting salary:** $22,000
**Training program:** None
**Internships:** Paid internships are held over the
  summer in media, account services, creative and
  research.
**Number of interns:** 3
**Personnel contact:** Lyn-Marie Schachtel

## N.W. AYER AND PARTNERS

Worldwide Plaza
825 Eighth Avenue
New York, NY 10019
212-474-5000
212-474-5400 (fax)

**Employees:** 500
**Annual billings:** $851,900,000
**Number of entry-level positions:** Few
**Job types:** Administrative assistants
**Average starting salary:** $16,000–$17,000
**Training program:** None

**Internships:** Unpaid, over the summer
**Number of interns:** 3
**Personnel contact:** Donna Milch; agency advises
  juniors to write directly to the head of the
  department where they wish to work.

## BBDO WORLDWIDE

1285 Avenue of the Americas
New York, NY 10019
212-459-5000
212-459-6645 (fax)
www.bbdo.com

**Employees:** 5,798 (worldwide)
**Annual billings:** $1,330,100,000
**Number of entry-level positions:** 24, 12 in media
  and 12 in account management
**Job types:** Assistant media planners, assistant media
  buyers, assistant account executives
**Average starting salary:** $25,000 in account
  management, $23,000 in media
**Training program:** Media training program in
  November and an account services program in
  February. Agency recruits at colleges and consor-
  tiums.
**Internships:** Unpaid internships during the summer
  and semester
**Number of interns:** 12
**Personnel contact:** Ron Mason

## BATES USA

The Chrysler Building
405 Lexington Avenue
New York, NY 10174
212-297-7000
212-986-0270 (fax)

**Employees:** NA
**Annual billings:** $5,111,521,000
**Number of entry level positions:** 40
**Job types:** Administrative assistants, assistant media
  planners, junior art directors/copywriters,
  assistant account executives (usually promoted
  from media)
**Average starting salary:** Media-$18,000; administra-
  tive assistants-$20,000–$22,000; junior art
  director/copywriter-$20,000.
**Training program:** In account management for
  MBA grads
**Average starting salary:** Mid $30,000s.

**Internships:** Both paid and unpaid internships are offered during the summer and a few during the year in media and research. None are available in account management.
**Number of interns:** 15
**Personnel contact:** Anne Melanson

## BERENTER GREENHOUSE & WEBSTER

233 Park Avenue South
New York, NY 10003
212-995-9500
212-995-9836 (fax)
www.bgw.com

**Employees:** 46
**Annual billings:** $78,000,000
**Number of entry level positions:** 1
**Job types:** Assistant media planner
**Average starting salary:** $18,000–$20,000
**Training program:** None
**Internships:** Paid interns are taken during the summer and the year in all departments as needed.
**Number of interns:** 4–5
**Personnel contact:** Margaret Heagney

## BIEDERMAN, KELLY & SHAFFER

475 Park Avenue South, 15 Floor
New York, NY 10016
212-213-5500
212-213-4775 (fax)

**Employees:** 40
**Annual billings:** $60,000,000
**Number of entry-level positions:** 1 every 2 years
**Average starting salary:** NA
**Training program:** None
**Internships:** The agency tries to accommodate all requests.
**Number of interns:** 2–3
**Personnel contact:** Kim Czander

## BOZELL WORLDWIDE, INC.

40 West 23rd Street
New York, NY 10010-5201
212-727-5000
212-727-2436 (fax)

**Employees:** 500
**Annual billings:** $610,000,000
**Number of entry-level positions:** 7
**Job types:** All departments
**Average starting salary:** $17,000–$19,000
**Training program:** In all departments including creative
**Internships:** No set program, usually unpaid and during the summer
**Number of interns:** 2
**Personnel contact:** Joanne Conforti

## DDB NEEDHAM

437 Madison Avenue
New York, NY 10022
212-415-2000
212-415-3562 (fax)
www.ddbn.com

**Employees:** 470
**Annual billings:** $76,815,000
**Number of entry-level positions:** 20
**Job types:** Administrative assistants, assistant media planners, assistant account executives
**Average starting salary:** $18,000–$25,000
**Training program:** None
**Internships:** Unpaid internships available throughout the year
**Number of interns:** 30
**Personnel contact:** Judson Saviskas

## DENTSU CORPORATION OF AMERICA

666 Fifth Avenue
New York, NY 10103
212-397-3333
212-397-3322 (fax)

**Employees:** 85
**Annual billings:** $13,735,775,000 (worldwide)
**Number of entry-level positions:** 6
**Job types:** Account assistants: some clerical, some account work.
**Average starting salary:** $20,000

**Training program:** None
**Internships:** Unpaid internships are available over the summer
**Number of interns:** 1
**Personnel contact:** Leslie Engel

## DEUTSCH, INC.

215 Park Ave. S.
New York, NY 10003
212-995-7500
212-353-9659 (fax)

**Employees:** 214
**Annual billings:** $379,500,000
See Deutsch/Los Angeles; Contact Kristin Greeves in the LA office for internship and employment inquiries.

## DOREMUS & CO.

200 Varick Street
New York, NY 10014
212-366-3000
212-366-3636 (fax)

**Employees:** 100
**Annual billings:** $100,000,000
**Number of entry-level positions:** 5
**Job types:** All
**Average starting salary:** $18,000–$22,000
**Training program:** None
**Internships:** Available in account management, creative, media, and production. Programs are offered occasionally during the summer and the year and are both paid and unpaid.
**Number of interns:** NA
**Personnel contact:** Laura Ari

## FERRELL CALVILLO COMMUNICATIONS

250 Park Avenue South
New York, NY 10003
212-777-0666
212-777-3261 (fax)

**Employees:** 45
**Annual billings:** $105,689,000
**Number of entry-level positions:** 3
**Job types:** Two administrative assistants, 1 assistant media planner
**Average starting salary:** Under $30,000

**Training program:** None
**Internships:** None
**Personnel contact:** Rita Sullivan

## FRANKFURT BALKIND PARTNERS

244 E. 58th St.
New York, NY 10022
212-421-5888
212-759-9284 (fax)
www.frankfurtbalkind.com

**Employees:** 90
**Annual billings:** $140,000,000
**Number of entry-level positions:** 12
**Job types:** Account management, design, technology
**Average starting salary:** Up to $30,000
**Overtime:** For certain positions
**Training program:** No
**Internships:** Year-round in account management, design, technology; pay depends on experience
**Number of interns:** 3–4
**Internship contact:** Janet Lee; jlee@frankfurtbalkind.com
**Personnel contact:** Same

## CLIFF FREEMAN AND PARTNERS

375 Hudson St.
New York, NY 10014
212-463-3200
212-463-3225

**Employees:** 125
**Annual Billings:** $250,000,000
Division of Saatchi & Saatchi

## GIRGENTI, HUGHES, BUTLER & MCDOWELL

100 Avenue of the Americas
New York, NY 10013
212-966-0077
212-966-7755 (fax)
Specialty: Healthcare/Over-the-counter products

**Employees:** 121
**Annual billings:** $190,000,000
**Number of entry-level positions:** 2
**Job types:** Account services; college grads usually start higher than administrative assistants.
**Average starting salary:** Low to mid $20,000s
**Training program:** None

**Internships:** Paid and unpaid internships are offered during the summer in all departments. Agency tries to accommodate requests.
**Number of interns:** 3
**Personnel contact:** Fran Davi

## GOTHAM, INC.

260 Madison Ave.
New York, NY 10016
212-213-4646
212-213-6710 (fax)
www.gothaminc.com

**Employees:** 100
**Annual billings:** $271,600,000
**Number of entry-level positions:** 7–10
**Job types:** Account coordinator, assistant media planner, junior art director, traffic, administrative
**Average starting salary:** Depends on job and experience
**Overtime:** For certain jobs
**Training program:** No
**Internships:** Occassionally, as warranted by work load in account services; paid and unpaid during summer and year
**Number of interns:** 2
**Internship contact:** Kim Randall; kimr@gothaminc.com
**Personnel contact:** Same

## GRACE & ROTHSCHILD

114 Fifth Ave.
New York, NY 10011
212-366-1600
212-989-0681 (fax)
www.gandr.com

**Employees:** 62
**Annual billings:** $141,790,000
**Number of entry-level positions:** 4
**Job types:** Account planners
**Average starting salary:** NA
**Overtime:** For jobs paying under $30,000
**Training program:** No
**Internships:** Infrequently; unpaid; result from internal referals
**Number of interns:** 2
**Internship contact:** NA
**Personnel contact:** Raena Bergstein; bergsteinr@gandr.com

## GREY ADVERTISING

777 Third Avenue
New York, NY 10017
212-546-2000
212-546-2584 (fax)
www.grey.com

**Employees:** 1,800
**Annual billings:** $1,959,000,000
**Number of entry-level positions:** NA
**Job types:** Assistant media planner, assistant account executive, junior buyers
**Average starting salary:** $20,000–$30,000
**Overtime:** No
**Training Program:** Account managment, media
**Internships:** Paid internships in media department during summer
**Number of interns:** 20
**Internship contact:** Mary Clare McNamee
**Personnel contact:** Mallory Anhouse

## GRIFFIN BACAL, INC.

130 Fifth Avenue
New York, NY 10011-4340
212-337-6300
212-645-0618 (fax)
www.gbinc.com

**Employees:** 235
**Annual billings:** $270,080,000
**Number of entry-level positions:** 50
**Job types:** Group assistants (account management), assistant media planners
**Average starting salary:** $18,000+ overtime
**Training Programs:** Not formal
**Internships:** College juniors can intern in account management over the summer
**Number of interns:** 4
**Personnel contact:** Mary Cioffi

## J. WALTER THOMPSON

466 Lexington Avenue
New York, NY 10017
212-210-7000
212-210-7078 (fax)

**Employees:** 370
**Annual billings:** $873,000,000
**Number of entry-level positions:** 15

**Job types:** Assistant account executive, assistant media planner, associate brand planner, junior creatives, assistants in direct marketing

**Average starting salary:** Mid to high $20,000s

**Overtime:** No

**Training program:** Professional development training is a cross-disciplinary, six-month program that involves classroom work, project work, and case studies; some departments have additional training on top of this program.

**Internships:** Held in all departments, including direct marketing, during the summer. Internships are paid, structured, and simulate a real job; students attend seminars and participate in projects.

**Number of interns:** 15

**Internship contact:** Seth Wolk; seth.wolk@jwalter.com

**Personnel contact:** Same

## JORDAN, McGRATH, CASE & TAYLOR

445 Park Avenue
New York, NY 10022
212-326-9100
212-326-9226 (fax)

**Employees:** 320

**Annual billings:** $510,000,000

**Number of entry-level positions:** 30

**Job types:** Assistant media planners, assistant account executives, a few administrative assistants

**Average starting salary:** $20,000–$28,000

**Training program:** None

**Internships:** Paid internships in all departments depending on need of agency, May through August and during winter and fall, depending on student's schedule.

**Number of interns:** 10

**Personnel contact:** Ms. Chris Martin

## KIRSHENBAUM BOND & PARTNERS

145 Avenue of the Americas
New York, NY 10013
212-633-0080
212-463-8643 (fax)

**Employees:** 96

**Annual billings:** $201,632,000

**Number of entry-level positions:** 15

**Job types:** All departments

**Average starting salary:** $17,000–$21,000

**Training program:** None

**Internships:** Students can intern during the summer in every department including creative and graphic design. Payment is by hourly wage or bonus.

**Number of interns:** 10

**Personnel contact:** Alice Oberman

## KOREY KAY & PARTNERS, INC.

130 Fifth Avenue
New York, NY 10011
212-620-4300
212-620-7149 (fax)

**Employees:** 48

**Annual billings:** $78,200,000

**Number of entry-level positions:** 5–10

**Job types:** Account coordinators, administrative assistants in creative and new business, audio visual assistants

**Average starting salary:** $18,000–$20,000

**Training program:** None

**Internships:** Students can intern during the summer in departments as needed. They are reimbursed for commuting costs.

**Number of interns:** NA

**Personnel contact:** Cindy Harwin

## LOIS/EJL

40 West 57th Street
New York, NY 10019
212-373-4700
212-586-9472 (fax)

**Employees:** 91

**Annual billings:** $390,000,000

**Number of entry-level positions:** 5

**Job types:** Assistant account executives, junior creatives

**Average starting salary:** $17,000–$19,000; $20/hr. for freelance creatives

**Training program:** None

**Internships:** None

## THE LORD GROUP

810 Seventh Avenue
New York, NY 10019
212-408-2100
212-957-9512 (fax)

**Employees:** 92
**Annual billings:** $145,191,000
**Number of entry-level positions:** 4
**Job types:** Assistant media planners, assistant account executives, administrative assistants
**Average starting salary:** Varies
**Training program:** For full-time junior employees in all departments
**Internships:** Students can intern during the summer in account management and are paid at a nominal rate.
**Number of interns:** 2
**Personnel contact:** Mercedes Colon

## LOTAS MINARD PATTON MCIVER

152 West 57th Street
New York, NY 10019
212-333-5676
212-333-5018 (fax)

**Employees:** 50
**Annual billings:** $80,125,000
**Number of entry-level positions:** 0
**Training program:** None
**Internships:** Paid internships in media and account management are available during the summer
**Number of interns:** 2
**Personnel contact:** Suzanne Conway

## THE LOWE GROUP

1114 Avenue of the Americas
New York, NY 10105
212-403-6700
212-403-6710 (fax)

**Employees:** 450
**Annual billings:** $575,000,000
**Number of entry-level positions:** 4–5
**Job types:** Administrative assistants
**Average starting salary:** "Very low," less than $20,000
**Training program:** None
**Internships:** None
**Personnel contact:** Ms. Pat Peltola

## MERKLEY NEWMAN HARTY

200 Varick St.
New York, NY 10014
212-366-3500
212-366-3637 (fax)
www.mnh.com

**Employees:** 125
**Annual billings:** $144,734,000
**Number of entry-level positions:** 10
**Job types:** Media, account services
**Average starting salary:** $22,000
**Overtime:** Yes
**Training program:** No
**Internships:** Summer in media, account services; paid
**Number of interns:** 3
**Internship contact:** Rhonda Steeg
**Personnel contact:** Same

## MESSNER VETERE BERGER MCNAMEE SCHMETTERER

350 Hudson Street
New York, NY 10014
212-886-4100
212-886-4415 (fax)

**Employees:** 200
**Annual billings:** $809,000,000
**Number of entry-level positions:** 10
**Job types:** Assistant media planners, assistant account executives; no administrative assistants
**Average starting salary:** $20,000s
**Training program:** None
**Internships:** None
**Personnel contact:** Debbie Breslin

## MEZZINA/BROWN

401 Park Ave. S.
New York, NY 10016
212-251-7700
212-532-3616 (fax)
www.mezzbrown.com

**Employees:** 100
**Annual billings:** $135,452,000
**Number of entry-level positions:** 20

**Job types:** Assistant media planner, assistant account executive, junior copywriter, assistant art director, administrative secretary
**Average starting salary:** $25,000
**Overtime:** NA
**Training program:** No
**Internships:** 6–8 weeks during summer; in traffic, creative, graphic services; paid
**Number of interns:** 6
**Internship contact:** Margaret Williams; mwilliams@mezzbrown.com
**Personnel contact:** Same

## OGILVY & MATHER

Worldwide Plaza
309 West 49th Street
New York, NY 10019
212-237-4000
212-237-5123 (fax)
www.ogilvy.com

**Employees:** 600
**Annual billings:** $1,396,506,000
**Number of entry-level positions:** 10
**Job types:** All
**Average starting salary:** Low $20,000s
**Training program:** Media and account training are available for students during the summer.
**Internships:** Paid internships are available during the summer in media, account services and creative.
**Number of interns:** 15
**Personnel contact:** Patricia Enright

## PARTNERS & SHEVACK

1211 Avenue of the Americas
New York, NY 10036
212-596-0200
212-354-1002 (fax)
www.partners-shevack.com

**Employees:** 125
**Annual billings:** $275,600,000
**Number of entry-level positions:** 3
**Job types:** Administrative assistants
**Average starting salary:** $21,000
**Training program:** None
**Internships:** Paid internships are available in all departments during the summer
**Number of interns:** NA
**Personnel contact:** Susan Scaglione

## PEDONE & PARTNERS

100 Fifth Ave., 4th Fl.
New York, NY 10011
212-627-3300
212-627-3966 (fax)

**Employees:** 43
**Annual billings:** $89,000,000
**Number of entry-level positions:** 0
**Training program:** None
**Internships:** None
**Personnel contact:** Diane Montpelier

## PUBLICIS/BLOOM

304 East 45th Street
New York, NY 10017
212-370-1313
212-984-1695 (fax)
www.p/b.com

**Employees:** 310
**Annual billings:** $145,000,000
**Number of entry-level positions:** Less than 5
**Job types:** Depends on need; occasionally hire assistant account executives
**Average starting salary:** NA
**Training program:** None
**Internships:** Students can intern occasionally for credit only during the semester or summer.
**Number of interns:** 3
**Personnel contact:** Fran Claff

## SAATCHI & SAATCHI ADVERTISING

375 Hudson Street
New York, NY 10014-3620
212-463-2000
212-463-3303 (fax)
www.saatchiny.com

**Number of Employees:** 500
**Annual billings:** $1,415,100,000
**Number of entry-level positions:** 18
**Job types:** Assistant media planner, assistant account executive, junior copywriter/art director
**Average starting salary:** NA
**Overtime:** No
**Training program:** Management training for all entry-level employees, yearly for 3–4 months
**Internships:** None

Personnel contact: Maureen Iannuzzi;
miannuzzi@saatchiny.com
Please send resumes to the attention of Human
Resources

## SUDLER & HENNESSEY

1633 Broadway
New York, NY 10019
212-969-5800
212-969-5991 (fax)

Number of Employees: 142
Annual billings: $168,000,000
Number of entry-level positions: 4
Job types: Traffic and media, promotable to assistant
account executive.
Average starting salary: NA
Training program: In-house training for junior
employees
Internships: None
Personnel contact: Rosa Lombardo

## TBWA/CHIAT DAY

292 Madison Avenue
New York, NY 10017
212-804-1000
212-840-1200 (fax)

Employees: 1,200 (worldwide)
Annual billings: $529,000,000
Number of Entry-level positions: 5–8
Job types: All, especially assistant media planners
and assistant account executives.
Average starting salary: NA
Training program: None
Internships: Mostly in account services, some in
creative and media; internship consists of a series
of seminars on different topics held for 10 weeks
from mid-June to mid-August. Some are paid,
most are unpaid.
Number of interns: 10–12
Personnel contact: Mia Salibello

## WARING & LAROSA

909 Third Avenue, 18th Floor
New York, NY 10022
212-755-0700
212-644-6980 (fax)

Employees: 75
Annual billings: $115,000,000
Number of entry-level positions: 2–3
Job types: All are receptionists or mail clerks,
promotable to account management or creative
Average starting salary: NA
Training program: None
Internships: Informal, during the summer, in any
department for which there is a need. Decisions
made in May
Number of interns: 2 at most
Personnel contact: Roberta Tucker

## WARREN/KREMER/CMP

Advertising, Inc.
2 Park Avenue
New York, NY 10016
212-686-2914
212-686-5652 (fax)

Employees: 44
Annual billings: $37,000,000
Number of entry-level positions: 3
Job types: 2 assistant account executives, 1 assistant
media planner
Average starting salary: $18,000–$20,000
Training program: None
Internships: Unpaid internships are offered during
the summer; students act as floaters and are
exposed to all departments
Number of interns: 1

## WARWICK BAKER O'NEILL

100 Avenue of the Americas
New York, NY 10013
212-941-4200
212-941-4277 (fax)

Employees: 125
Annual billings: $850,348,000
Number of entry-level positions: 3
Job types: Assistant media planners, assistant
account executives, administrative assistants; very
hard to get into creative

Average starting salary: $18,000–$21,000

Training program: Nothing formal, but agency does send junior people to programs at the Ad Club and to a 16-week IAAS spring training program sponsored by the 4A's

Internships: Usually in account management or new business, media and creative when available. Available during the summer and year, both paid and unpaid

Number of interns: 4 during summer, 2 during year

Personnel contact: Michelle Peterson or Ann Demeri

## WELLS RICH GREENE BDDP

9 West 57th Street
New York, NY 10019
212-303-5000
212-303-5040 (fax)

Employees: 302

Annual billings: $846,600,000

Number of entry-level positions: 20

Job types: All are administrative assistants

Average starting salary: $18,000

Training program: Throughout the year for junior people in account services and media

Internships: There are occasional paid summer internships in account services.

Number of interns: 3–4

## WILLIAM DOUGLAS MCADAMS, INC.

1740 Broadway
New York, NY 10019
212-698-4000
212-698-4003 (fax)

Employees: 208

Annual billings: $196,200,000

Number of entry-level positions: 6

Job types: 5 administrative assistants in all departments; 1 account coordinator with 1–2 years experience

Average starting salary: $20,000–$25,000

Training program: None

Internships: Summer (paid) and semester (unpaid) internships are offered in account services, marketing, creative and sometimes research.

Number of interns: NA

Personnel contact: Bill Young

## WUNDERMAN CATO JOHNSON

675 Avenue of the Americas
New York, NY 10010
212-941-3000
212-941-3652 (fax)

Employees: 415

Billings: $1,638,000,000

Number of entry-level positions: 25

Job types: Administrative assistants in all departments

Average starting salary: $20,000

Training program: In all departments once you are hired

Internships: None

Personnel contact: Judy Magnus-Jackson

## YOUNG & RUBICAM, INC.

285 Madison Avenue
New York, NY 10017
212-210-3000
212-490-9073 (fax)
www.yr.com

Employees: NA

Annual billings: $9,900,000,000

Number of entry-level positions: Varies from year to year

Job types: Varies from year to year

Training program: Account management training program offered to MBAs during the summer; send resumes in January

Internships: Summer (paid) and semester (unpaid) internships in media and account services are offered.

Number of interns: 20

Personnel contact: Virginia Hancher

# ASSOCIATIONS — NEW YORK

## THE ADVERTISING CLUB OF NEW YORK

235 Park Avenue South, 6th Floor
New York, NY 10003
212-533-8080

The Advertising Club comprises all segments of the advertising profession, from account executives to those in creative, media planning, research, and traffic.

Monthly luncheon programs and seminars provide insight into current trends and feature an array of activities.

The Club has a Young Professionals Division for members under thirty years of age, which accounts for one third of club memberships. The $50.00 membership fee entitles members to an *Adweek* subscription and invitations to all monthly events, seminars, and other functions, some of which are free. This division has its own Board as well as educational programming and social committees. Through these committees, members have the opportunity to work on pro bono advertising campaigns (current projects include the American Cancer Society's Great American Smokeout, Drugs Don't Work, and Women's Action Alliance), plan networking parties, and organize social events.

The Ad Club Foundation awards grants to high school and undergraduate students, sponsors "Junior Ad Clubs," administers a summer internship program that places about thirty interns in New York agencies, hosts a creative advertising competition and matches younger professionals with industry leaders in a Mentor Program. In addition, the Club sponsors Advertising & Marketing 101, a lecture course taught by advertising experts.

## THE ADVERTISING RESEARCH FOUNDATION

641 Lexington
New York, NY 10022
212-751-5656
www.urfsite.org

The members of this foundation include advertisers, agencies, media companies, and research firms whose goal is to advance the science and practice of advertising research. They do not offer any career guidance to students interested in the field, but they will often let graduate students use the Foundation's library.

## ADVERTISING WOMEN OF NEW YORK

153 East 57th Street
New York, NY 10022
212-593-1950

Advertising Women of New York (AWNY) was founded in 1912 and today consists of 720 members and 50 junior members. These women hold executive positions in advertising, marketing, merchandising, promotion, public relations, and media. Their common goals are to improve the status of women in the communications industry, promote equal opportunity by developing members' professional skills, and contribute to the growth of young professionals. AWNY offers junior memberships to women under the age of twenty-five for $50.00/year. There are separate meetings for juniors and a mentoring program. AWNY publishes a monthly newsletter and hosts seminars, events, and luncheons each month (there are additional charges for these). There are two free events per year. In November AWNY sponsors the College Career Conference, which draws five to six hundred students (both men and women) and recent college grads. The $65.00 fee covers a weekend of networking, workshops, portfolio reviews, and keynote speakers.

## AMERICAN ADVERTISING FEDERATION

1225 Connecticut Avenue, NW
Washington, DC 20036
1-800-999-2331

The American Advertising Federation (AAF) is "the only national association encompassing and representing all aspects and disciplines of the advertising industry." It is headquarted in Washington, D.C., and has 52,000 members.

Its academic division has 200 chapters in universities across the country and 6,000 student members. The AAF College World Series of Advertising is an annual advertising competition in which college chapters take a corporate case study and develop a marketing plan, advertising campaign, and media strategy. College teams compete within their division and the finalists compete at the AAF National Conference. The winning team presents its campaign to conference attendees, including ad industry and corporate executives. Many students receive job offers from agencies as a result of their participation in this highly esteemed competition.

Student AAF members receive five issues of the *Communicator* newsletter and the annual *AAF Internship Directory* listing of more than 1,000 advertising internships across the country. They also have access to advertising videotapes and directories through the AAF library, and students can reach the Education Services Department toll free (1-800-999-AAF1).

AAF sponsors an annual National Advertising Conference open to everyone involved or interested in the industry. Nationally recognized industry leaders present workshops and speeches on key issues. Highlights include a Career Search seminar led by advertising recruiters and a creative, hands-on, mini-ad campaign workshop.

AAF's "Ad 2" club is a nationwide network of clubs providing activities and programs designed for young professionals in advertising under the age of thirty-one. Monthly programs feature prominent speakers in the industry and offer an opportunity to network with established professionals. Members can also participate in producing a full-scale public service campaign for a nonprofit organization, including research, tv, radio, print production, and public relations. Finally, Ad 2 members have access to a job bank with connections to potential employers. For information, contact AAF Education Services at 1-800-999-AAF1.

The AAF Foundation offers two internship programs for college students:

The Milt Gossett Creative Advertising Workshop places a multicultural selection of college juniors in a three-day intensive workshop at some of New York's top advertising agencies, such as J. Walter Thompson, Saatchi & Saatchi, and Bozell Worldwide. The Vance Stickell Memorial Internship Program chooses outstanding advertising students for 10-week paid summer internships.

The AAF is also starting a mentoring program to offer guidance to minorities who are just beginning their advertising careers. Contact Heide Gardner, AAF manager of diversity and strategic programs, at 1-800-999-2231; hgardner@aaf.org

## AMERICAN ASSOCIATION OF ADVERTISING AGENCIES

(known as the 4As)
666 Third Avenue
New York, NY 10017
212-682-2500

Founded in 1917, members of the 4A's now include 550 agencies in the U.S. and abroad. Their objective is "to promote and further the interests of advertising agencies by increasing their usefulness to advertisers, to the media, and to the public." The association's committee on education and employment publishes career guides for students. The publications department has a listing of booklets, most of which cost $2.00. The Association also sponsors the Minority Advertising Internship Program, placing forty or fifty interns in agencies across the country. Twenty to twenty-five of these placements are in New York City. All internships are paid, and students can apply to particular departments within their agencies of choice.

## THE ART DIRECTORS CLUB

250 Park Avenue South
New York, NY 10003
212-674-0500

There are currently 400 student members and 600 regular members in this club. Student membership is $35.00. The club offers an annual scholarship to a junior in an art school in the New York metropolitan area and schedules six portfolio review sessions during April and May, open to seniors in any school. It also hosts monthly events with a nominal fee and publishes a quarterly newsletter.

## THE CLIO ORGANIZATION

276 Fifth Avenue, Suite 401
New York, NY 10001
212-683-4300

This group sponsors the annual Clio festival, which includes a student category of awards. The application deadline is April 15. Awards are given in television, radio, print, and packaging categories.

## DIRECT MARKETING EDUCATIONAL FOUNDATION

6 East 43rd Street
New York, NY 10017
212-768-7277 ext. 335
www.the-dma.org

The Direct Marketing Educational Foundation (DMEF) is a nonprofit sister organization of the Direct Marketing Association that provides education and vocational training for students and professors. It sponsors the collegiate ECHO Competition for college students to act as an ad agency by teaming up to develop a marketing strategy, budget, creative campaign, and media plan based on the challenge of a corporate sponsor.

Leading direct marketing professionals offer an intensive, professional, four-day seminar in direct marketing basics sponsored by The Collegiate Institute. A program notice is sent to professors who then select eligible students to apply to the Foundation, and the DMEF holds competitions for juniors and seniors throughout the year to qualify. The Institute is a competitive program, usually offered three times a year to twenty or thirty students. The only cost is the first $150 of transportation expenses. The DMEF also circulates the resumes of these students to 100 companies.

Graduate students with limited experience in direct marketing can also participate in a weekend seminars covering direct marketing fundamentals, applications, key issues, and a case project. The only cost to students is the first $150 of transportation expenses.

The DMEF holds an internship program for 8-10 weeks during the summer. Opportunities are listed in the DMEF's *Directory of Direct Marketing Summer Internships*. Each listing includes a job description and requirements, a contact name, deadlines, and information about how to apply.

## THE ONE CLUB

32 East 21st Street
New York, NY 10010
212-979-1900

The One Club is strictly for copywriters, art directors and "wannabes." The club offers free lectures and seminars to its 650 members. Junior membership is free the first year and $45.00 the following year. Four portfolio reviews are held throughout the year for members of any level. Events and showings are great places to rub shoulders with the senior folks—all aspiring creatives should contact this club.

## PROMOTION MARKETING ASSOCIATION OF AMERICA

257 Park Ave. S.
New York, NY 10010
212 420-1100
www.pmaalink.org/html/mainscrn.html

This association offers education and information about the promotions field. Its academic membership allows students to attend the four annual conferences and monthly educational seminars at a reduced rate.

# RECRUITERS—NEW YORK

## ALPERT EXECUTIVE SEARCH

Graybar Building
420 Lexington Ave., Ste. 2024
New York, NY 10170
212-297-9009
Alpertsearch@wordlnet.att.net
Contact: Ada Alpert

Ada Alpert specializes in placing account planners, but it's a tough market for juniors, she says. Most agencies will not pay a fee to a recruiter to find a junior employee, but every once in a while, a job does cross her desk. There are not many junior level jobs because planners must develop an understanding of the advertising process and the creative development process, credibility with creative directors, and an ability to identify an idea that is relevant to execution of an ad. All this, of course, takes some time.

The best way to break into planning is to come in as junior researcher where you will learn to set up focus groups, work with vendors for questionnaire design, and begin to understand how the consumer thinks and feels. Some agencies such as Young & Rubicam, Kirshenbaum & Bond, Wells BDDP, and Deutsch do have beginning-level planners. But jobs are few and far between and reserved for only the best and brightest. Many agencies are beginning to recognize the need to train junior planners and some are starting in-house programs on an individual basis.

Planning is about how you think and how you identify ideas, says Ada. Planners are very intuitive and highly creative, yet they think in divergent ways. They are able to work effectively with a range of different people and they have the credibility and confidence to develop a rapport and communication within a team. Planners are just as significant as the creative and account team; they are partners in the creative, strategic, and decision-making process. Planners can have very diverse backgrounds, seemingly non-related to advertising, though psychology, sociology, and anthropology are certainly helpful. Successful planners combine logic with creative thinking, and it's an unusual person who embodies all these characteristics.

Planning is being embraced across the country; it is a key function in New York agencies as well as Los Angeles and San Francisco. Chicago is still in a growth phase. Agencies in other cities such as Fallon McElligot, Wieden and Kennedy, The Martin Agency, GSD&M and The Richards Group have also been at the forefront of planning.

Read everything you can about advertising and planning, Ada recommends, including: *Under the Radar: Talking to Today's Cynical Consumer,* by Jonathan Bond and Richard Kirshenbaum; *Disruption: Overturning Conventions and Shaking Up the Marketplace,* by Jean-Marie Dru; *Hitting the Sweet Spot: How Consumer Insights Can Inspire Better Marketing and Advertising,* by Lisa Fortini-Campbell; *Truth, Lies and Advertising,* by John Steel.

## DALE CUNNINGHAM AGENCY

14 East 60th Street
New York, NY 10022
212-223-0277
Contact: Phyllis Cunningham

This agency deals with creative placements for assistant art directors and copywriters. It also places entry-level traffic, talent payment, and print production positions. There are occasional openings for assistant account executives.

## FORUM PERSONNEL

342 Madison Avenue
New York, NY 10017
212-687-4050
Contact: Karen Katz, VP

Forum handles entry-level jobs in market research, media (assistant planners), traffic, creative (junior art directors), and graphic arts.

## LIZ GLATZER & ASSOCIATES

420 Lexington Ave., Ste. 300
New York, NY 10170
212-297-6160

Liz Glatzer works with candidates with as little as one year experience who are looking for junior positions in advertising, such as assistant account executive, or perhaps moving from media into account services. Liz looks at a person as a package, and seeks out particular qualities, such as intellectual curiosity and a passion for the advertising business and for selling products. "Do as much informational interviewing and networking as you can," she recommends. Internalize the industry's common ideas and jargon; learn to talk about why you like a product from a marketer's standpoint as opposed to describing a commercial you think is funny; show *how* you think as opposed to *what* you think, she says. And make sure you use plenty of other mechanisms to get a job, from your alumni network to friends and family.

## ROZ GOLDFARB ASSOCIATES, INT'L (RGA)

23 East 22nd Street, 3rd Floor
New York, NY 10010
(212) 475-0099

Roz Goldfarb Associates specializes in advertising, design, and corporate communications and is grounded in "civilized headhunting." RGA International's advertising department places copywriters, art directors, and account executives in all ranges of positions, from entry level to management. The agency also handles positions in traffic and production, marketing, administration, planning, and new business development. RGA clients include advertising agencies, direct marketing agencies, sales promotion firms, and corporations with in-house advertising and communications departments.

## JERRY FIELDS ASSOCIATES

353 Lexington Avenue
New York, NY 10016
212-661-6644
Contact: Phil Growick

This agency specializes in entry-level jobs in creative and account management for approximately sixty New York agencies and branch offices; contact them six months before graduation. The agency also reviews portfolios for junior copywriters and art directors and places them in jobs or internships.

## REMER-RIBOLOW & ASSOCIATES

230 Park Avenue, Suite 222
New York, NY 10169
212-808-0580
Contact: Dawn Rasmussen

Places administrative assistants in account management, strategic services, and market research. They often have positions for assistant account executives, assistant media planners and buyers, and new business development assistants.

## SMITH FIFTH AVENUE AGENCY

17 E. 45th Street
New York, NY 10017
212-682-5300

Places people with at least three years of advertising experience.

## JUDY WALD AGENCY

210 E. 60th St.
New York, NY 10022
212-421-6750

Judy Wald says that she only deals with students coming out of the "advertising schools" (School of Visual Arts, Pratt School of Design), but sounds like she could be swayed by a bright young person with strong internship experience.

# AGENCIES—SAN FRANCISCO

## ANDERSON & LEMBKE

2 Harrison St., 7th Fl.
San Francisco, CA 94105
415-543-8080
415-543-8088 (fax)
www.anderson-lembke.com

**Employees:** 150
**Annual billings:** $81,000,000
**Number of entry-level positions:** 35
**Job types:** Media, account service, account planning, traffic, creative
**Average starting salary:** $28,000

**Overtime:** Depending on position
**Training program:** No
**Internships:** Account service, creative, media; year-round, paid
**Internship contact:** Brian Waldman; brian_waldman@anlsf.com
**Personnel contact:** Same

## CITRON HALIGMAN BEDECARRE

1160 Battery St.
San Francisco, CA 94111
415-705-0100
415-705-0150 (fax)
www.chbnet.com

**Employees:** 60
**Annual billings:** $100,000,000
**Number of entry-level positions:** 3
**Job types:** Administrative, creative, planning
**Average starting salary:** $21,000
**Overtime:** Yes
**Training program:** No
**Internships:** Year-round in all departments; participates in Inroads Minority Internship Program; paid
**Number of interns:** 3
**Internship contact:** Pamela Boyes; pamela_boyes@chbnet.com
**Personnel contact:** Same

## COHN & WELLS

909 Montgomery St., Ste. 300
San Francisco, CA 94133
415-705-6600
415-705-6624 (fax)

**Employees:** 65
**Annual billings:** $280,000,000
**Number of entry-level positions:** 5
**Job types:** Production, account management, administrative
**Average starting salary:** NA
**Training program:** In development
**Internships:** Account management, strategic planning, studio, depending on need; year-round, paid
**Internship contact:** Kimber Patterson; kpatterson@cohn-wells.com
**Personnel contact:** Same

## DDB NEEDHAM SAN FRANCISCO

170 Maiden Lane, 3rd Fl.
San Francisco, CA 94108
415-732-3600
415-732-3636 (fax)
www.ddbn.com

**Employees:** 45
**Annual billings:** $8,100,000,000
**Number of entry level positions:** 4
**Job types:** Account services
**Average starting salary:** High $20,000s to low $30,000s
**Overtime:** No
**Training program:** No
**Internships:** Depending on need; unpaid
**Number of interns:** 1
**Internship coordinator:** Suzanne Collins; sue.collins@sf.ddbn.com
**Personnel contact:** Same

## EVANS GROUP

160 Pacific Ave., Ste. 200
San Francisco, CA 94111
415-398-2669
415-398-1043 (fax)
www.evansgroup.com

**Employees:** 70
**Annual billings:** $290,000,000
**Number of entry-level positions:** Unknown
**Job types:** Account coordinator, media assistant, publicity assistant (in entertainment division), associate art director
**Average starting salary:** NA
**Overtime:** No
**Training program:** No
**Internship:** Public relations, entertainment, advertising—account services, media, production; held in summer and year-round; some are paid
**Number of interns:** 5–6 in summer
**Internship contact:** Advertising: Sonya Shemdin; Entertainment: Sasha Lord
**Personnel contact:** David Meighan

## FRANKEL & COMPANY

731 Sansome St., 5th Fl.
San Francisco, CA 94111
415-263-7700
415-434-4727 (fax)
www.frankel.com

**Employees:** 35
**Annual billings:** $320,000,000
See Chicago office listing

## HAL RINEY & PARTNERS

735 Battery St.
San Francisco, CA 94111
415-981-0950
415-955-4389 (fax)
www.hrp.com

**Employees:** 350
**Annual billings:** $475,000,000
**Number of entry-level positions:** NA
**Job types:** All departments
**Average starting salary:** NA
**Training program:** No
**Internships:** Held for 10 weeks from June to August
    in all departments; paid
**Number of interns:** NA
**Internship contact:** Kristin Stein
**Personnel contact:** Mary Kelly

## INGALLS MORANVILLE ADVERTISING

530 Bush St., Ste. 501
San Francisco, CA 94108
www.imad.com

**Employees:** 23
**Annual billings:** New agency
**Number of entry-level positions:** NA
**Job types:** Coordinator positions
**Average starting salary:** $20,000–$25,000
**Overtime:** Yes
**Training program:** No
**Internships:** Creative and account services during
    summer, various other throughout year; paid
    stipend
**Number of interns:** 5
**Internship contact:** Liza Dyer; liza_dyer@imad.com
**Personnel contact:** Same

## MCCANN-ERICKSON/SAN FRANCISCO

201 California St.
San Francisco, CA 94111
415-616-6000
415-981-2523 (fax)

**Employees:** 155
**Annual billings:** $7,927,600,000
**Number of entry-level positions:** NA
**Job types:** All departments
**Average starting salary:** NA
**Overtime:** Yes
**Training program:** No
**Internships:** No
**Personnel contact:** Kathryn Kluegel

## WINKLER MCMANUS

150 Spear St., 16th Fl.
San Francisco, CA 94105
415-957-0242
415-495-7118 (fax)
www.winklerad.com

**Employees:** 65
**Annual billings:** $60,000,000
**Number of entry-level positions:** 5
**Job types:** Media assistant, account coordinator,
    receptionist
**Average starting salary:** NA
**Training program:** No
**Internships:** No
**Personnel contact:** Andrea Hackett

## YOUNG & RUBICAM SAN FRANCISCO

100 First St.
San Francisco, CA 94105
415-882-0600
415-896-0533 (fax)

**Employees:** 175
**Annual billings:** $9,900,000,000
**Number of entry-level positions:** 10
**Job types:** Account management, account planning,
    production, creative
**Average starting salary:** low $20,000s
**Overtime:** Yes
**Training program:** Account management, media,
    year-round

**Internships:** Year-round in all departments; paid and unpaid

**Internship contact:** Whitney Ball; whitney_ball@yr.com

**Personnel contact:** Same

# ASSOCIATIONS—SAN FRANCISCO

## THE SAN FRANCISCO ADVERTISING CLUB

150 Post Street, Suite 325
San Francisco, CA 94108
415-986-3878
415-986-0357, 24-hour Event Hotline
www.sfadclub.com
Contact: Steve Chipman

The San Francisco Ad Club is one of the largest and most active communications organizations in the San Francisco Bay Area, consisting of over 800 professionals and reflecting every facet of the advertising community. Its web site features job openings as well as a comprehensive list of agencies in the San Francisco area.

The Club offers monthly luncheon programs with speakers, networking and social events, creative showcases, competitions, and more; some events focus on specialized segments of the industry, such as interactive technology.

The Club also provides programs for college students, such as an annual Ad Education Career Day, and offers student scholarships and internships for advertising and marketing majors. Recent college grads can join the Ad2 division geared to professionals younger than thirty-one.

Media Mania is the Ad Club's hardcore media training program. For eleven weeks, top media directors and representatives from leading agencies share their knowledge on launching a successful media career. Classes cover all aspects of media planning, research and buying. Call the Ad Club office for an application.

## AMERICAN ADVERTISING FEDERATION

251 Post St., Ste. 302
San Francisco, CA 94108
415-421-6867
www.arf.org

## ADMARK: THE EAST BAY AD CLUB

415-546-9181
www.admark.org

AdMARK's mission is "to act as a unifying voice for the area's advertising professionals...while supporting education, diversity, and worthwhile causes and recognizing creative excellence, all in a warm and enjoyable environment."

Monthly programs and special events supplement AdMARK's professional development seminars, panels, and special monthly programs to keep young professionals on top of the latest trends and ideas. Internship listings are available through the office as well as online. Regular meetings are held on the third Tuesday of each month and begin with an 11:30 a.m. mixer, followed by a noon lunch and program, held at Scott's Seafood Restaurants.

## THE ACCOUNT PLANNING GROUP

www.apgsf.org

The Account Planning Group (APG) of San Francisco currently consists of the ten planning directors at those San Francisco agencies where account planning is established. Their goal is to raise the profile of account planning on the West Coast and help raise account planning standards with training programs in San Francisco.

APG events are open to everybody, including account planners, creatives, media people, account management, and clients; the group meets on the second Monday of every month at various agencies.

## AMA, SAN FRANCISCO BAY AREA CHAPTER

P.O. Box 27278
San Francisco, CA 94127
(415) 994-242
www.sfba-ama.org

The San Francisco Bay Area Chapter of the American Marketing Association (AMA) has about 750 members. The group operates a job bank, linking job seekers and prospective employers by matching qualified applicants with positions. Resumes sent to the Job Bank by job seekers are filed according to job objectives and level of experience, and those matching job descriptions are passed on to the appropriate employer, who independently contacts job seekers who are most qualified for the position. Over 125 resumes are currently on file, and an average of ten requests are filled per month. Listings include everything from marketing coordinator and research assistant to director of marketing, and everything in between.

The AMA also publishes *Career Watch*, a monthly newsletter that features job listings.

Contact the Job Bank at:

Socratic Technologies
3850 25th street, SF, CA 94114
415-648-2802

# GENERAL ADVERTISING RESOURCES

## DIRECTORIES

### Advertising and Communications Yellow Pages

New York Yellow Pages
113 University Place
New York, NY 10003
212-675-0900

### Adweek's Directory of Advertising

BPI Communications, Inc.
1515 Broadway
New York, NY 10036
212-764-7300

Regionalized series of books containing information on agencies and advertisers.

### Directory of Market Researchers

(also known as the Green Book)

The American Marketing Association
60 E. 42nd Street
New York, NY 10017
212-557-3825

### Encyclopedia of Associations

Gale Research
835 Penobscot
Detroit, MI
1-800-877-8238

### Standard Directory of Advertising Agencies

National Register Publishing, New Providence, NJ (also known as the advertising *"Red Book"*). Lists 9,000 agencies and their annual billings, billings by media, number of employees, key personnel, and accounts; also features a section of cyberagencies. Other publications in the series include the *Standard Directory of Advertisers* and the *Standard Directory of International Advertisers and Agencies.*

## BOOKS

*Advertising: Principles and Practice,* John Burnett, Sandra E. Moriarty, William D. Wells. Prentice Hall, 1995.

A textbook with a real-world focus. Includes examples, issues, and applications interlaced with both the theory and practice of advertising.

*Advertising and Popular Culture,* Jib Fowles. Sage Publications, 1996.

Reflecting current theories, this critique uses excerpts from advertising campaigns to illustrate how modern advertising draws from and contributes to popular culture.

*The Art Direction Book.* (D&Ad Mastercraft Series). Rotovision, 1997.

*The Art of Writing Advertising: Conversations with William Bernbach, Leo Burnett, George Gribbin, David Ogilvy, Rosser Reeves,* Denis Higgins, ed. National Textbook Company, 1986.

*Copywriting by Design: Bringing Ideas to Life with Words and Images,* David Herzbrun. NTC Business Books, 1997.

*Media Planning: A Practical Guide,* Jim Surmanek. NTC Publishing Group, 1995.

Concise explanations of complex concepts and terms help readers understand every aspect of media planning. In addition to featuring traditional techniques, the book highlights new media terminology and explains how technologies will affect today's media planner.

*The One to One Future: Building Relationships One Customer at a Time,* Don Peppers, Martha Rogers. Doubleday, 1997.

Describes the "one-to-one" marketing paradigm.

*The World's Greatest Brands,* Nick Kochan, ed., New York University Press, 1997.

Stories behind the most successful brands and the reasons for their success. Examines the way branding works, how successful branding can be achieved, and the latest trends in branding.

# PART FOUR

## Appendix

## MAGAZINES

### Advertising Age

Crain Communications
740 Rush St.
Chicago, IL 60611
800-678-9595

### Adweek

ASM Communications
P.O. Box 1974
Danbury, CT 06813
800-722-6658

### American Demographics

127 W. State St.
Ithaca, NY 14851
800-350-3060

### Brandweek

ASM Communications
P.O. Box 1974
Danbury, CT 06813
800-722-6658

### Business Marketing

Crain Communications
740 N. Rush St.
Chicago, IL 60611
800-678-9595

### Communication Arts

Coyne & Blanchard
PO Box 10300
Palo Alto, CA 94303
415-326-6040

### Journal of Advertising Research

The Advertising Research Foundation
3 East 54th St.
New York, NY 10022
212-751-5656

### Journal of Marketing and Journal of Marketing Research

American Marketing Association
250 South Wacker Dr.
Chicago, IL 60606
1-312-648-0536

### Marketing Communications

Media Horizons
50 West 23rd St., 6th Fl.
New York, NY 10010
212-645-1000

### Marketing News

American Marketing Association
250 South Wacker Dr.
Chicago, IL 60606
312-993-9517

### Television and Radio Age

Television Editorial Corp.
1270 Avenue of the Americas
New York, NY 10020
212-757-8400

## ONLINE RESOURCES

### Ad agency directory

www.volition.com/agency.html

### ARDEN

www.arden-inc.com

ARDEN is the Automated Resource Data Entry Network, an interactive database containing resumes, job listings (including entry-level positions), and internships for people seeking employment in advertising. The site is linked to the home page of the American Association of Advertising Agencies, so 620 top agencies have the opportunity to post jobs and review candidates' credentials. ARDEN costs $15.00/month for database access.

### Jobs in advertising

www.monster.com/jobs/
advertising_employment.htm

**Jobs in marketing**

www.marketingjobs.com

**Links to advertising associations**

www.commercepark.com/aaaa/
member_services/
media_related_links.html

**Links to marketing associations**

www.marketingjobs.com/mktassoc.html

**Latest industry news**

www.adtalk.com

**The University Of Texas At Austin, Department Of Advertising**

www.advertising.utexas.edu/world

is one of the most extensive collections of advertising-related links on the Web

# DIRECT MARKETING RESOURCES

## DIRECTORIES

*The Direct Marketing Market Place: Directory of the Direct Marketing Industry.* National Register Publications, New Providence, NJ

## BOOKS

*Beyond 2000: The Future of Direct Marketing,* Jerry I. Reitman, ed. NTC Publishing Group, 1994.

*Direct and Database Marketing,* Graeme McCorkell. Kogan Page Ltd., 1997.

*Direct Marketing : An Integrated Approach,* William J. McDonald. Richard D. Irwin, 1997.

*Direct Marketing Through Broadcast Media: TV, Radio, Cable, Infomercials, Home Shopping, and More,* Al Eicoff. NTC Publishing Group, 1995.

Comprehensive coverage of all of the newest media forms and techniques, written by a pioneer of broadcast direct marketing.

*The New Integrated Direct Marketing,* Mike Berry. Gower Publishing Co., 1998.

*2,439 Tested Secrets for Direct Marketing Success: The Pros Tell You Their Time-Proven Secrets,* Denny Hatch, Donald Jackson. NTC Business Books, 1997.

*Winning Direct Response Advertising: From Print Through Interactive Media,* Joan Throckmorton. NTC Business Books, 1997.

*Write on Target: The Direct Marketer's Copywriting Handbook,* Donna Baier Stein, Floyd Kemske. NTC Business Books, 1997.

## MAGAZINES

**Catalog Age**

11 Riverbend Dr. S.
P.O. Box 4949
Stamford, CT 06907
203-358-8523

**The Cowles Report on Database Marketing**

11 Riverbend Dr. S.
P.O. Box 4949
Stamford, CT 06907
203-358-9900

**DM News**

Mill Hollow Corporation
100 Avenue of the Americas, 6th Floor
New York, NY 10013
212-741-2095

**Direct**

Cowles Business Media
11 Riverbend Dr. S.
PO Box 4949
Stamford, CT 06907
203-358-9900

**Direct Marketing Magazine**

Hoke Communications
224 7th St.
Garden City, NY 11530
516-746-6700

**Journal of Database Marketing**

Henry Stewart Publications
North American Business Office
810 E. 10th St., PO Box 1897
Lawrence, KS 66044
913-843-1221

## Premium/Incentive Business

Gralla Publications
1515 Broadway
New York, NY 10036
212-869-1300

## Response TV

Advanstar Communications
201 E. Sandpoint Ave.
Santa Ana, CA 92707
714-513-8400

## Target Marketing

North American Publishing Co.
401 N. Broad St.
Philadelphia, PA 19108
215-238-5300

### ONLINE RESOURCES

**Direct Marketing World's Job Center**

www.dmworld.com/jobcenter/jobs.html

**Direct Marketing News**

www.mediacentral.com/Magazines/
DirectNewsline

**Direct Marketing World**

www.dmworld.com

# ETHNIC ADVERTISING RESOURCES

### BOOKS

*Advertising and Marketing to the New Majority/A Case Study Approach,* Gail Baker Woods. Wadsworth Publishing, 1994.

*Hispanic Market Handbook: The Definitive Source for Reaching This Lucrative Segment of American Consumers,* M. Isabel Valdes, Marta H. Seoane. Gale Research, 1995.

Conveys the fundamental differences that distinguish Hispanic-American consumers from mainstream American consumers.

*Successful Marketing to U.S. Hispanics and Asians: Players, Agencies, and Media: An American Management Association Research Report on Target Markets,* AMACOM, 1987.

*Target: The U.S. Asian Market: A Practical Guide to Doing Business,* Angi Ma Wong. Pacific Heritage Books, 1993.

Covers demographics, segments, marketing language and strategies, successful selling techniques, pricing, etiquette, and more.

### ONLINE RESOURCES

**Trends in marketing to the Pacific Rim**

www.asiacentral.com

# INTERACTIVE ADVERTISING RESOURCES

### BOOKS

*Advertising on the Internet,* Robbin Zeff, Bradley Aronson. John Wiley & Sons, 1997.

Describes what advertising on the web is about, from banner ads and beyond, from an advertiser's point of view.

*Enterprise One to One: Tools for Competing in the Interactive Age,* Don Peppers, Martha Rogers. Doubleday, 1997.

Explains how to harness technology to achieve competitive advantages in customer loyalty, retain customers, and increase the share of each customer's business.

*Interactive Marketing: The Future Present,* Edward Forrest and Richard Mizerski, eds. NTC Business Books, 1996.

Chapters include customer-focused strategies, interactive retailing, marketing high-tech products, disk-based marketing communications, interactive selling, copyrighting for interactive media, web advertising, measuring the effectiveness of interactive marketing, and more.

*The Internet Advertising Report,* Mary Meeker, Morgan Stanley. HarperCollins, 1997.

Profiles some of the best Internet ads and emerging web companies today and addresses key issues in interactive advertising.

**Marketing on the Internet,** Jill H. Ellsworth, Matthew V. Ellsworth. John Wiley & Sons, 1996.

Reveals latest trends in electronic commerce and covers latest technological developments including Java, VRML, Shockwave, and ActiveX.

**Publicity on the Internet: Creating Successful Publicity Campaigns on the Internet and the Commercial Online Services,** Steve O'Keefe. John Wiley & Sons, 1996.

A hands-on, nuts-and-bolts book full of forms, checklists, sample publicity campaigns, online resources, and expert strategies accumulated from Steve O'Keefe's 5+ years in the cyber-publicity world.

**Strategic Internet Marketing,** Tom Vassos. Que Education & Training, 1996.

Provides case studies and specific advice for implementing a marketing plan along with strategies for advanced and interactive web site design.

**What Makes People Click: Advertising on the Web,** Jim Sterne. Que Education & Training, 1997.

## MAGAZINES

**Electronic Media**
> Crain Communications
> 740 N. Rush St.
> Chicago, IL 60611
> 1-800-678-9595

**Interactive Services Report**
> P.O. Box 28022
> Washington, DC 20038

**Internet World**
> Mecklermedia Corp.
> 20 Ketchum St.
> Westport, CT 08860
> 1-800-573-3062

**Journal of Interactive Marketing**
> John Wiley & Sons
> 605 Third Ave.
> New York, NY 10158
> 212-850-6000

**The Web**
> PC World Communications
> 501 Second St., #500
> San Francisco, CA 94107

**Wireless Week**
> Chilton Publishing Group
> 825 Seventh Ave.
> New York, NY 10019
> 212-887-8560

## ONLINE RESOURCES

**The Internet advertising discussion list**
> www.exposure-usa.com/i-advertising/

**Discussion group for advertising and marketing on the Internet**
> tnn.marketing.internet

**Interactive media news and links to journals**
> www.mediacentral.com

**Internet Advertising Bureau**
> www.iab.net

**List of interactive agencies across the country**
> www.netsurf.com/nsf/v01/02/resource/ad.html

**Association for Interactive Media**
> www.interactivehq.org

**Silicon Alley News**
> www.news-ny.com

# MEDICAL ADVERTISING RESOURCES

## BOOKS

**The Best Medical Advertising and Graphics Selections from the Rx Club Show,** Joseph Fatton, ed. Rockport Publishing, 1993.

**The Medical Marketing Plan/Book and Disk,** Stuart C. Rogers, Richard H. Thompson Jr. Irwin Professional Publishing, 1992.

## MAGAZINES

**Med Ad News**
> Engel Communications
> 820 Bear Tavern Road
> West Trenton, NJ 08628
> 609-530-0044

**Perspectives, Trends in Health Care Marketing**

CPS Communications
31 Bailey Ave., PO Box 488
Ridgefield, CT 06877
203-438-9301

# SALES PROMOTION RESOURCES

## BOOKS

*Advertising and Sales Promotion Strategy,* Gerald Tellis. Addison-Wesley Publishing, 1997.

*Dartnell Sales Promotion Handbook,* Tamara Brezen Block and William A. Robinson, eds. Dartnell Corp.,1994.

A good reference book detailing all aspects of the sales promotion industry

*The Only Sales Promotion Techniques You'll Ever Need,* Tamara Block, ed. Dartnell Corporation, 1997.

*Promotion Marketing,* William A. Robinson and Christine Hauri. NTC Business.

Details the challenges of promotional marketing through a chronological history starting in the 1950s. The last section looks to the future.

*Promotional Marketing : Ideas and Techniques for Success in Sales Promotion,* William A. Robinson, Christine Hauri. NTC Publishing Group, 1995.

*Sales Promotion Essentials: The 10 Basic Sales Promotion Techniques...and How to Use Them,* Don E. Schultz, William A. Robinson, Lisa A. Petrison. NTC Publishing Group, 1993.

Complete, concise, easy to use, marketing bestseller covers the ten key sales promotion techniques and explains how each one works.

*Winning with Promotion Power,* Fran Caci and Donna Howard. Irwin/McGraw-Hill.

Provides a detailed analysis of 100 award-winning promotions from 1983-1993.

## MAGAZINES

**Incentive**

Bill Comunications
355 Park Ave. S.
New York, NY 10010
212-592-6358

Includes information on the incentive field, from premiums and travel to couponing, sweepstakes, and event marketing.

**Potentials In Marketing**

Lakewood Publications
50 South Ninth Street
Minneapolis, MN 55402
612-333-0471

Covers a range of subjects related to promotion marketing, with an emphasis on sales incentive products.

**Promo**

Cowles Business Media
11 Riverhead Dr. S.
Stamford, CT 06907
203-358-9900

News about major promoters geared to people who work for agencies. Heavy packaged-goods emphasis, but also coverage of other industries.

www.review.com

# Expert Advice

## Talk About It

www.review.com

## Pop Surveys

# Paying for it

www.review.com

# THE PRINCETON REVIEW

www.review.com

# Getting in

## Word du Jour

www.review.com

# Find-O-Rama School & Career Search

# www.review.com

## Best Schools

# Finding it

www.review.com

# FIND US...

## International

### Hong Kong
4/F Sun Hung Kai Centre
30 Harbour Road, Wan Chai,
Hong Kong
Tel: (011)85-2-517-3016

### Japan
Fuji Building 40, 15-14
Sakuragaokacho, Shibuya Ku,
Tokyo 150, Japan
Tel: (011)81-3-3463-1343

### Korea
Tae Young Bldg, 944-24,
Daechi- Dong, Kangnam-Ku
The Princeton Review- ANC
Seoul, Korea 135-280,
South Korea
Tel: (011)82-2-554-7763

### Mexico City
PR Mex S De RL De Cv
Guanajuato 228 Col. Roma
06700 Mexico D.F., Mexico
Tel: 525-564-9468

### Montreal
666 Sherbrooke St.
West, Suite 202
Montreal, QC H3A 1E7 Canada
Tel: (514) 499-0870

### Pakistan
1 Bawa Park - 90 Upper Mall
Lahore, Pakistan
Tel: (011)92-42-571-2315

### Spain
Pza. Castilla, 3 - 5° A, 28046
Madrid, Spain
Tel: (011)341-323-4212

### Taiwan
155 Chung Hsiao East Road
Section 4 - 4th Floor,
Taipei R.O.C., Taiwan
Tel: (011)886-2-751-1243

### Thailand
Building One, 99 Wireless Road
Bangkok, Thailand 10330
Tel: (662) 256-7080

### Toronto
1240 Bay Street, Suite 300
Toronto M5R 2A7 Canada
Tel: (800) 495-7737
Tel: (716) 839-4391

### Vancouver
4212 University Way NE,
Suite 204
Seattle, WA 98105
Tel: (206) 548-1100

## National (U.S.)

We have over 60 offices around the U.S. and
run courses in over 400 sites. For courses and locations
within the U.S. call 1 (800) 2/Review and you will be
routed to the nearest office.